MW00573521

A Hip Hop Pedagogy:
Effective Teacher Training for the Millennial Generation

Carol A. O'Connor, PhD

Foreword by Aaron R. Ireland

Edited by SaFiya D. Hoskins, PhD

DEDICATION

This study is dedicated to the members of the global hip hop community. You have inspired me. May this serve as a contribution to the acknowledgement and respect you so richly deserve, and to the betterment of communities through education.

CONTENTS

ACKNOWLEDGMENTS

With gratitude and humility I would like to acknowledge and thank Dr. Neari Warner, Dr. Joseph M. Stevenson, Dr. Wynetta Lee, Dr. LaVerne Gentry, and Dr. Walter Crockett. It goes without saying that I could not have done this without you all.

Giving a very special thanks to Dr. SaFiya D. Hoskins.

I would also like to thank Aaron R. Ireland.

1 FOREWORD

I remember the first time I heard Boogie Down Productions and KRS-1. I was at a friend's house party, I was in the 8th grade and the song was *Stop the Violence*. The people in the party were very familiar with the tune and sang the chorus in unison. They loved the song so much. They were all smiling while they sang and it made me instantly love and want to discover more about the song and artist (yes, I missed the release of Criminal Minded and "the first album cover"). That same year I'd purchased two turntables, a tuner, a mixer and a speaker so that I could be a DJ like my older cousin. Soon after the party I went to the record store and purchased the Boogie Down Productions album, *By Any Means Necessary*, where you will find the song, *Stop the Violence*.

My father took me to the record store and then followed me up to my room to play the song on my record player. We listened to the lyrics: "1-2-3! The crew is called BDP! And if you want to go to the tip-top! Stop the violence in hip hop! WHYYYY OOOOH!"

"YES!" I thought, "I got the right album and now I own the song and can become familiar with it like my buddies!" Then my father asked me, "What does he mean by 'Hip Hop'?" Dismissively I replied, "I don't know?" I wanted him to leave me alone and let me enjoy my new record. But no, I thought about what 'Hip Hop' meant. I could not figure it out. Then he told me. Yes, I am admitting publicly as a proud Hip Hop child, that my father "put me up" on Hip Hop... HE told ME!

My father said, "Remember that song? The first rap song? It went 'Hip Hop, hibbit, a hibbit to the hip hip hoppa ya don't stoooop!'"

"Yes!" Of course I remembered Sugar Hill Gang's *Rapper's Delight*, and it was indeed the first rap song we had ever heard. He went on to explain that rap music is probably 'Hip Hop' because of that song. I am not sure whether the culture was defined that early and named 'Hip Hop' because of *Rapper's Delight* but what definitely happened was that my father became engaged in "my music." He pushed me to first listen to the lyrics and not just the beat or the chorus. Secondly, my father drove me to think critically about what those lyrics meant and what the lyricist intent may have been as he scribed those lyrics.

I remember the push to play Hip Hop on the major radio stations. It was tough. We had to play tapes to hear our favorite raps, and then the songs they did eventually play on the radio were the "sell out" raps. Commercial rap. Impure. Rappers were, as Dr. Dre and NWA put it, "scared to use profanity when up on the microphone." This would eventually change as radio moved towards adopting an all Hip Hop/ rap format with R&B sprinkled in. Now, in 2016, some who grew up on Hip Hop and longed for the day when "their" music would be played in mainstream radio programming are fighting to have it removed from the radio playlists. We have seen a movement from the revolutionary to the gangster. From "out go the weaves, in go the braids beads medallions" to "now she's a gangster." Conscious to controlled. To quote Dr. Dre again, in the song *Let Me Ride* he waxes that rap went from "medallions, dreadlocks and black fists" to "just that gangster glare."

As a teacher in Chicago, I have noticed that one of the main obstacles we have to traverse in our attempt to align our students with their academic success is the influence of the media and specifically the music that is played on radio stations marketed towards marginalized citizens, pigeon-holed many, the disadvantaged or whatever we are calling us now. Marginalized me can remember playing "Ghetto Boyz" and becoming hyped up to fight if necessary as my high school buddies and I drove to a party at a "foreign" school. No lie. Music got us charged up.

As a young and impressionable boy from the suggested/ recommended/ less frowned upon two parent home, I have experienced the influence first handedly. Today students are bombarded with messages of marginalization. Too many songs portray women as strippers or otherwise promiscuous, money-hungry gold diggers, and men as gangsters, drug dealers and misogynistic brutes, and both as mindlessly materialistic and easily influenced. If one identifies a problem and does nothing to fix it, they are simply complaining. If they make strides towards righting a wrong, they are an activist. In college we were always guided away from being what my Africana Studies department head, Dr. Al-Hadid, called "arm chair revolutionaries." So, naturally, I formed with like-minded individuals who felt the same about the music on the radio to change the playlist and offer some balance. Are there no current artists who make positive lyrics? Certainly. I play them all the time but they get no spins on radio. We even met with executives at a local radio station and expressed our concerns. The radio executive explained that their programming reflects the demands of the demographic. It became clear that the channels established for us to voice our concerns (as we reached out to and protested corporate sponsors of the station and wrote letters to the FCC about the offensive content being forced upon our community in an attempt to have the content reviewed and ultimately addressed) were not interested in changing the playlist on stations marketed towards minorities.

We formed a 501(c) 3 to answer social imbalances and injustices and to fight against those inequalities. We began to collaborate with others on a curriculum that would address our concerns. Our approach is through media in general and more specifically through a critical analysis of the lyrical content played on stations marketed towards minorities. We created a curriculum that discusses media literacy and at the end of each class we have a lyric read-along where we dissect the popular lyrics of the day. We ask students to discuss the themes of the song and to write about what the lyrics inspire them to do/ become.

I see many who grew up on music from the "golden era" of Hip Hop being dismissive towards ("dissing") the lyrics and artists of today. Do we not see how we ushered in the general acceptance of such lyrics? If my father would have spoken ill about KRS-1 I

3

would have listened more just to spite him. And although KRS is a "conscious" rapper and it is hard to speak ill about his lyrical content (Can you tell that I'm a fan?), the guidance of an experienced person listening with me made my experience richer. But today's artists provide ample subjects that can be discussed and *must* be discussed with mature guidance. We must begin to analyze lyrics with our students/ children. Uncensored and alongside.

Parents- do you know what molly is? How about the 'bando? More than likely your high school student does. Shouldn't you know what is influencing your child's behavior or entering your child's thoughts? What is painting their world and defining their potential? There is generally more influencing your child than just the guidance of a parent/ guardian.

By listening alongside and uncensored, we can demystify adulthood by showing youth how we maturely navigate through a world where we are aware of the same influences but choose to engage in behaviors that will bring success rather than death. We demonstrate a balance that sometimes manifests as moderation rather than abstinence. It is at this point that Hip Hop becomes a tool through which we can cultivate critical thought. It takes us into the business world, supply and demand. Give the people what they want. Discussions of social justice, art, culture and life arise. Pontification on the music industry and the structure of corporations. The proliferation and use of Hip Hop in advertising and marketing- that industry and their influence. Career choices. We become advocates, an ally, consultants who inform and expand the awareness and therefore the potential of our student/ child. We have witnessed a change in what is popular among Hip Hop. Gangster rap has gone from being a voice of the marginalized to a marketing tool for the prison industrial complex. Our "searching for a way out of a reserved hell" children who have fallen "in love with the coco" are choosing to be "fresh as hell" even if the "feds watchin'." These lyrics are a subliminal affirmation to encourage the unsuspecting listener of lesser developed critical thought to do away further with critical thought- rendering them an empty vessel to carry out any actions, behaviors and thoughts injected into their zombie-like unconsciousness.

Using Hip Hop and media in general as a pedagogical tool we can meet our youth where they are and encourage them to think critically about their world. We are teaching about grit when we should also be teaching about getting a grip on that which is influential to our students. We often hear about how successful members from impoverished areas become successful and subsequently move to more affluent areas leaving the ghetto bereft of positive images which is all too often coupled with the daddy deficit. Devoid of role models. My father was a black pharmacy student in the 50s and always said and I quote, "The reason I became a pharmacist is because the dude across the street was a pharmacist and he had a baaad ride and a gorgeous bride." Hey, he was young.

We must educate from that which influences the student. For some it is love, the opposite sex- which could also translate into wanting to start a family, for some it is money, helping people, for others it is simply the want of having fun and partying all the time. There are mature ways for a child to move into these ways of life after they have secured their future. We have to begin to teach how much more fun life is when you can travel with friends and/ or lovers! And how much fun it is NOT to be of an age where you can legally do these things and be restricted by economic misfortune resulting from a lack of vision and drive as a young adult. Life doesn't really get super fun until 25 (when you can rent a car in Miami or any other city) and that kick is way better than the "kick back" party always going on to distract you from your youthful studies. Which is better? Critical thought is required to weigh the options. Hip Hop provides subject matter like that which I have mentioned here and much more.

Our ability to change begins with our belief system. Influential people affect our belief system and when they look like us, research shows that we tend to faster believe that we too can be influential/ successful. If those models are positive then our self-image will be affected positively as well. Hip Hop has assumed the role of influence for an unbalanced many in disadvantaged communities.

Research reflects the importance of equipping a student with the ability to critically define their world and themselves in that world. Why would a student choose to sell/ use drugs, crack credit cards, steal cars or rob if they knew that learning to code or program a computer could earn them a monthly salary that most people work 1-2 years for? And they could still buy property in their own name and live sans the stress and fear of being "caught by the feds" and use the money they earn to take care of themselves when they are old? Who, besides one who displays an insufficient understanding of concepts such as "delayed gratification" or "emotional intelligence" would choose a life of crime? The schools in impoverished areas do not display curricula that cultivate the attributes of a leader. Through Hip Hop we can teach a student about media influences and how this industry has helped influence mass genocide, politics, general attitudes towards groups of people and wars. But also positive things like developments in science and technology, or what aspects of a platinum selling recording artist make that artist a leader? We can also inform activism, highlight the dangers of living a 'thugs life,' and the importance of viewing the world through a global lens because they know of Tupac from Trenton, NJ to Tanzania.

We are seeing children march into jail and justify the acts that got them on that path. All too often I meet students who have been taught (by grandmothers at times-ages of academic abuse) to do what is "smart" instead of what is "right." If you were raised by a family who has been given illusions of choice since their arrival in your town (or to America for that matter) and though they may be smarter or more able than their status quo representative, they are forced to live in a culture of poverty.

When you realize that you have been pigeon holed into a marginalized way of life, among other attitudes you may get angry or lethargic, you may develop a laser-like focus on your academics, or you may choose to fit that mold that has been defined for you. You may begin to believe that robbing someone to feed your child is your best option. One may begin to truly believe that the quick money earned in the drug market or any other underworld scheme is the smart path to take.

This speaks to a diminished value judgment system and critical point of view. Who is to take care of your child or your family if you get caught and incarcerated? How much will it now cost your family to accept phone calls or to drive to visit or to feed you from the commissary? Why are so many choosing jails over college? Where does the desire to live outside of our means develop? Where is that desire strengthened? I offer Hip Hop as both a problem and a solution and since both perspectives cancel the other we can argue that Hip Hop itself is neutral. What becomes the impetus for change is the environmental influences or lack thereof. If there is no guidance, children will form their own rites of passage and guide each other with narrow scopes of global awareness. This is ghetto youth culture.

One concept that challenges generations is having the younger generation understand that the older generation is informed and the advice that is offered is for the benefit of the younger generation. The sayings, "been there done that" and "there is nothing new under the sun" if understood can add strength to a mentor relationship. Additionally, it is important for the older generations to understand that the youth have a voice and agency. It is important for that older/ seasoned/ experienced generation to not belittle the perspectives of the youth because there are some "new" concepts that will develop and should be dissected, understood accepted and applied. The mentor relationship is a sensitive two way street.

This is a very interesting time for Black America. We are seeing a generation who does the same things as their parents. For instance, my father did not play video games nor did he listen to Hip Hop. For him it was Monopoly, Jazz and Classical music. But here we are, a generation of adults and children who listen to the same music and play video games! What a great opportunity to sit with our children and discuss themes that arise in those mediums. We can ask, "What would happen if you stood in front of someone driving their car, made them stop, went to their window and yanked them through, and then drove off in a stolen vehicle? How much incarceration time would you be awarded? Who is paying your rent or feeding your family while you're in jail? If your rent is not paid where will you live when you get out?" Or we might ask, "What would happen if you got caught selling drugs at the 'bando?" We could challenge them to ponder, "How much more likely is it that you would go to jail if you walk and drive around with an unregistered pistol?" We can ask a child to describe an exotic dancer's pension plan and then ask about the popularity of this career in music marketed towards black people. We can ask a child to describe the attributes of a wife and a mother and juxtapose this with the images that arise when we listen to female rappers of the day.

What I see as most important is the development of honest dialogue between student and mentor (child and parent/ guardian/ teacher/ etc.). We can no longer afford to sugar coat content and conversation. Too many of the images and messages directed at our weakened societal links are harsh and heartless. The counter narrative has to be just as strong in our attempt to neutralize the potential negative effects. And we must stay anchored to our cause which is not to censor artists who are simply expressing themselves but to control radio content and where this is impossible, to create grassroots programs that will guide the community towards critically defining that which influences them in an attempt to choose their most positive and driven forms.

Aaron R. Ireland
Chicago, IL
12/31/2015

Aaron R. Ireland is the founder of LOTUS (Lifting Ourselves Through Us) a 501c3 organization that is committed to the global fight against academic and social inequality by creating curriculum content that speaks to and empowers marginalized citizens. Aaron is also an educator, having taught at several charter school networks in Chicago. He conducts media literacy workshops and serves as a mentor to students and young adults. Aaron was born and raised on Chicago's South Side and attended Chicago Public Schools from 1st through 12th grade, including Edgar Allan Poe Classical School and Whitney Young High School. He graduated from Tennessee State University with a BA in Africana Studies and is currently pursuing a master's degree at the University of Chicago's Urban Education Institute in the Urban Teacher Education Program.

What are the ramifications of taking hip-hop out of pedagogy?

If you don't know hip-hop, at least a little bit of it, you can't even
call yourself an American. So I don't even know who these
educators are who are ignoring basic American street life. In the
future, hip-hop is going to be called American folklore.

KRS-One
KRS-One Weighs in on 'Illegal'
Arizona 'Ethnic Studies' Class
RollingStone
February 9, 2015

CAROL A. O'CONNOR, PHD

2 A COMPLEX PROBLEM

This study initially focused on the self-perceptions of teachers regarding their preparedness for classroom work after their graduation from teacher training programs. The foundational research question for this study is as follows: How does formal teacher training prepare teachers to meet the educational needs of urban at-risk students? To investigate this and three other research questions 10 teachers and one former teacher were interviewed. Most of the teachers are employed in schools in large urban school districts, although one works in a rural location. The former teacher is an internationally known rap artist and actor. This was a qualitative study that utilized a phenomenological research methodology. The data were analyzed in terms of frequency of recurrent themes and interpreted in relation to the research questions. Most of the participants in this study reported that their pre-service training had inadequately prepared them for the realities encountered in their own classrooms. Most participants also stated that they had developed other techniques and approaches to instructional delivery based on elements of experiential knowledge gained subsequent to completion of their university training.

A theme that occurred regularly in the data was the efficacy of utilizing elements of hip hop culture to engage students through building on their prior knowledge and constructing lessons that students perceived as relevant to their own lives. Most teachers recommended the inclusion of hip hop awareness as an element of formal teacher training programs.

During the past several decades, concerns about the interrelatedness of teacher preparation, student achievement, and the quality of the American school system have grown in the United States (Cohen, 1998; National Center for Education Statistics, 2001). Some of the concerns that apply to teachers include: the type and level of degree held, content-area knowledge, knowledge of state and district standards, and the ability to address the needs of culturally and linguistically diverse students. These concerns frequently are addressed in discussions about specific student-related issues including drop-out rates, low reading ability, and poor levels of achievement on standardized tests. Disparities in student test scores have been noted among groups and have been attributed to factors such as ethnicity, race, gender, and socioeconomic class (Cohen, 1998; National Center for Education Statistics, 2001).

In response to these concerns, the federal government has enacted legislation aimed at rectification of these issues. The No Child Left Behind Act of 2001 (Bush, 2001) contains language that defines the criteria for the designation Highly Qualified Teacher, mandates increased levels of achievement for all students, and sets forth significant penalties for non-compliance. Members of the education community have struggled, with varying degrees of success, to meet these requirements. In numerous studies, teacher quality has been found to be the highest predictor of student achievement, and the issue of adequately prepared teachers is considered an essential element in attempts to meet the needs of all students (Caruthers, 2006; McKinney, Robinson, & Spooner, 2004; Whisnant, Elliott & Pynchon, 2005). This study examines some crucial factors influencing teachers' preparedness for meeting these important challenges.

Teachers in the public K-12 school system should be adequately prepared to meet the instructional needs of all students, including those from culturally and economically diverse backgrounds. Increasing numbers of students nationwide are minorities, and many of these students come from families facing recurrent financial and social challenges (Fass & Cauthen, 2007; NCCP, 2008; Payne 2005). The majority of public school teachers –

especially those working in urban schools and in low socioeconomic areas – report that they do not feel well enough prepared to address these at-risk students' educational needs (Huntley, 2008; National Center for Education Statistics, 2001; Rubenstein, 2007). Various facets of this complex problem have been widely addressed in the literature. The apparent lack of congruence between teacher preparedness and at-risk students' needs is important since it may have a significant impact on their educational attainment, employment prospects, and other future opportunities. Research indicates that well-prepared, highly qualified teachers are the most significant factor in a child's or young adult's school achievement (Boe, Shin, & Cook, 2007; McKinney, Robinson, & Spooner, 2004). Although a wide range of literature targets topics such as teacher preparedness, formal and experiential learning, characteristics of institutions, and student characteristics, there is little consensus regarding effective ways to bridge the gap between teacher preparedness and effective teaching of at-risk students (Berry & Norton, 2006; Caruthers, 2006). To date, several studies have examined the implications for practice situated within educational theories, and some of these have reported successful outcomes in terms of student engagement and achievement (Henderson-Sparks, Paredes, & Gonzalez, 2002; Reede & Black, 2006).

In order to meaningfully address the issue of teacher preparedness, it is important to note that researchers differ in the way they define, approach, and report on key concepts and terms. Preparedness, for example, is usually taken to mean that state of instructional expertise a teacher brings to the classroom, based on knowledge gleaned from formal instruction and other sources. Within such a definition other questions arise, such as the meaning and content of formal instruction, and whether other sources might provide insights and methods that would boost student achievement. In the current educational and political era, achievement is usually equated with demonstrating a specified level of proficiency on state-mandated standardized tests (Bush, 2001).

This single-minded focus on standardized test scores as the sole measure of a student's learning and a teacher's proficiency has come under harsh criticism from numerous sources; critics include teachers and administrators, parents, students, the business community, and other stakeholders. Complaints include: the arbitrary cut-off points for determining "passing" scores, the cultural bias inherent in the form of testing and in some of the test items, narrowing of the curriculum, and the relevance of successful test-taking in predicting readiness for the workforce, for higher education, and for other post-secondary options (Burke-Adams, 2007).

Student demographics are changing nationwide, and the number of minority students in the K-12 system is expected to register continued exponential growth (Payne, 2008). In many urban schools, so-called minorities comprise the majority, with middle-class white students sparsely represented. Research indicates that a generational component informs student characteristics as well (Coomes & DeBard, 2004). The millennial generation comprises students who have grown up with technology, and who usually far outpace their teachers in its use and application. These students also have been described as non-sequential learners, willing to plunge into tasks and experiment to find workable solutions. Studies have found that millennials are greatly influenced by mass media, including elements of hip hop culture, which serve a function in informing their identity (Coomes & DeBard, 2004; Dyson, 2007; Payne, 2008; Powell, 2006; Rose, 2008; Stovall, 2006).

This shift in student population has required both new and veteran teachers to expand their repertoire of teaching strategies and to devise new ways to maximize instructional effectiveness. Higher education instructors, school administrators and teachers have redesigned teacher induction programs, initiated or expanded mentoring programs, and set aside more time for teacher collaboration. Teachers have designed and implemented new approaches to content delivery, and schools have provided large numbers of teachers with induction and mentoring programs, as well as in-services and other professional development based on identified areas of school activity (Cherubini, 2006; Whisnant, Elliott, & Pynchon, 2005). Despite these measures, however, student scores in many academic areas remain at levels indicative of non-proficiency (NCES, 2001). Teachers report that most professional development activities have not helped them improve instruction, and the teacher attrition rate is appallingly high; as many as 50% of new teachers leave the profession within the first five years (Gonzales, Brown, & Slate, 2008). The cost of recruiting and training new teachers can be measured not only in terms of dollars, but also in loss of continuity in instructional programs, and disruption of faculty cohesiveness (Boe, Cook, & Sunderland, 2006; Gonzales, Brown, & Slate, 2008; Patton & Kritsonis, 2006).

The implications of these trends on students are manifested in lack of academic achievement, high dropout rates, and subsequent engagement in riskier activities, often followed by incarceration (Payne, 2005). Students who do not attain necessary knowledge and skills in school usually find only limited options for employment, almost invariably at the low end of the wage scale (Payne, 2005; Payne, 2008). The loss to the individual, to families, and to the community is significant in several areas. Lost or foregone earnings are only one factor in this equation; more damaging is the lack of the social and human capital development that would facilitate upward mobility (Cabrerra & La Nasa, 2000; Hossler, Schmidt, & Vesper, 1998; McDonough, 1997).

In addition to the loss of individual opportunity and potential, the societal costs of student non-achievement are enormous. These include the necessity of allocating larger portions of public funds to health care and the corrections system, which further exacerbates the problem of underfunding for schools, especially those most in need of additional resources. Society also will find itself increasingly pressured to meet its obligations, due to the lost productivity of a larger segment of the populace. This trend, if left unchecked, could result in diminished vigor of communities, states, and ultimately, of the nation.

The trends outlined above also impact higher education in numerous ways. Statistical data are available through federal government databases and other sources and serve as a backdrop for researchers' investigations. Researchers have viewed the implications addressed above from at least three perspectives: the effect on universities' current teacher training programs, the need to explore and develop new paradigms for university and school partnerships, and the effects of poorly prepared incoming students (Ahuja, 2007; Allen, 2003; Haberman, 2008; Thompson & Smith, 2005) .

Studies investigating current teacher training programs abound and may be divided into categories depending on the focus of the research. Although some quantitative studies were found, the majority of these investigations used a qualitative approach. According to the literature, there is evidence that some teacher-training programs still utilize an antiquated instructional paradigm with undue emphasis on theory and method without taking student characteristics and needs into account (Allen, 2003; Boe, Cook, & Sutherland, 2006; Giallo & Little, 2003). This fact is set forth in partial explanation for teachers' self-reported feelings of unpreparedness for the rigors encountered in the classroom. As accounts of mediocre teacher training programs have multiplied, the demand from government authorities for institutional accountability has increased as well, although these proposals have met with resistance. Nonetheless, accreditation procedures for teacher training programs have been put into place, and more than 652 colleges of education have been awarded certification (NCATE, 2001). The authenticity of the criteria for accreditation also is subject to debate.

Newer paradigms of teacher education have emerged, with the professional development model one of the more prevalent. Proponents of this approach to teacher training point out the long-term and close involvement of university faculty and teacher candidates with K-12 teachers and administrators; another salient feature of this model is the guided immersion of pre-service teachers in actual classrooms throughout the school year. Intended benefits of professional development schools include exposure of teacher candidates to actual classrooms and students, which, it is claimed, will make them better prepared for classrooms of their own. Data support the assertion that these candidates score higher on teacher-certification tests, although their effectiveness and persistence in the profession are inconclusive. This is one of many areas that warrants additional study.

As indicated above, research indicates that a generational component influences student characteristics as well. Studies have found that millennials are greatly influenced by mass media such as films, music and hip hop culture which serve a function in identity formation, lifestyle choices, and perspectives on critical areas of their lives (Caruthers, 2006; Comissiong, 2007; Coomes & DeBard, 2004; Dyson, 2007; Green, 2007; Hill, 2009, Stovall, 2006). For many students, especially minority urban youth, hip hop texts serve as a basis for the formation of notions of self within and outside of formal educational spaces (Hill, 2009; Jasper, 2009).

Another important shift in the focus of teacher training discussions is the move toward a willingness to make inquiry student-focused, rather than predominantly teacher-focused. Many of the areas described above provide fertile areas for additional qualitative and quantitative research. In addition to the political and legal mandates imposed by legislation by No Child Left Behind, there is a moral imperative to investigate and develop ways to best meet the needs of all students, especially those most in danger of truly being left behind.

The purpose of this qualitative study was to explore and gain understanding of factors contributing to the enhancement of teacher preparedness. Utilization of a narrative research design facilitated participants' discussions of teacher training programs and subsequent activities, both formal and experiential. Through interviews with current and former teachers, it was possible to gain insight into how preparedness for effective interaction with diverse students could be advanced. The input of teachers was elicited primarily at locations in Mississippi, although telephone interviews were conducted with participants in Arizona and Louisiana.

Research Questions

1.   How does formal teacher training prepare teachers to meet students' needs?
2.   How does experiential training affect teacher preparedness?
3.   How do the characteristics of students from diverse background impact teacher preparedness?
4.   What recommendations do teachers propose to inform practice and enhance preparedness?

The significance of this study lies in its likely contributions to policy, practice, and the amelioration of the harmful neglect of student needs. It also may result in the refinement of existing theories of learning, the generation of new theories, and may serve as a starting point for additional research in these areas (Marshall & Rossman, 2006). These contributions to the body of knowledge are expected to occur within a current societal context where greater accountability for performance and achievement is expected of students, teachers, and administrators (Bush, 2001).

The costs to schools and to society resulting from the inability of teachers to effectively meet the needs of diverse learners are enormous and must be viewed in terms of financial, personal, community and national impact. As teachers become discouraged by their inability to effectively interact with at-risk students, they may either transfer to another school, or leave the profession entirely; worse yet, they may sink into apathy and remain in their current position where they continue to neglect students who most need help and support. Fortunately, the latter type of teacher is rare, but addressing this issue in terms of providing all teachers with alternatives that engender hope and confidence is essential.

The examination of factors outlined in the problem statement above contributes to the national, state, and regional discussion about effective teacher preparation and its impact on the academic achievement of at-risk students. Illumination of this important teacher-student relationship was expected to be the most significant outcome of this investigation. Since the literature reveals that consensus in these areas is elusive, it was hoped that new information discovered during the data collection process would serve to help clarify issues surrounding the topic of teacher preparedness. In addition, educators seeking funding from government agencies and foundations will be able to utilize these findings to justify their need for projects that support teacher and student learning.

Implications for higher education policy may include adjustments to program design and delivery, the nature of partnerships with school districts, and the methods used to assess outcomes. Findings that add to the study and delivery of effective teaching practices are of interest to institution presidents and faculty, especially those involved with teacher preparation programs. Study findings also may play a valuable role in strategic planning activities (Bryson, 2004). Results of this study may be of interest across disciplines and serve as a focal point for interdisciplinary work. In addition, it is hoped that the study will serve as a basis for additional research and allow for the development of recommendations that will help colleges and universities provide teacher candidates, as well as new and veteran teachers, with the knowledge and strategies they will need to better help all students achieve.

Policy implications at the district, state and federal levels could be reflected in changes in legislative mandates that would shift the focus toward more holistic notions of achievement and accountability, and away from its currently punitive format. Rather than invoking the threat of sanctions such as teacher and administrator terminations and school closures (Bush, 2001), states could better allocate funding to provide for more teacher and student support in identified areas of need. Precluding further state incursions into areas where government policy conflicts with practitioner knowledge would be a productive outcome.

This was a qualitative study, based in a constructivist knowledge claim and utilizing a phenomenological approach (Creswell, 2003; Denzin & Lincoln, 2003; Marshall & Rossman, 2006). Through open-ended interview questions, participants were able to fully describe their perceptions, experiences, and ideas (Creswell, 2003; Creswell, 2008). This approach best fit investigation of the problem delineated above, since it allowed meaning to emerge during participant interviews (Cresswell, 2003; Denzin & Lincoln, 2003).

The study was based on a series of interviews with teachers at different grade levels. Participants were encouraged to express themselves fully and to add comments and observations as they deemed appropriate. The data gathered during this process were examined, and emergent patterns extrapolated and reported (Denzin & Lincoln, 2003; Wolcott, 1994). As Creswell (2008) predicted, new issues arose during participant interviews, which affected the shape and direction of the study (Creswell, 2008). The most notable of these was the predominance of references to hip hop pedagogy which was utilized in some manner by every interviewee.

Delimitations included the examination of teacher education programs as viewed through the perceptions of program graduates. A limited number of participants were selected on the basis of location and accessibility. The researcher chose locations based on familiarity with student demographics in those areas as well as the result of referrals. The opportunity to meet with participants was limited to one occasion, thereby magnifying the possibility for omissions and errors. To address this concern, follow-up procedures included telephone calls and email correspondence as needed for clarification and expansion of comments.

Another delimitation occurred as the result of unexpected difficulties in securing a sufficient number of participants. The researcher utilized snowball sampling, but had to augment this with recommendations from other sources outside the first chain generated through this technique. This, in effect, started another chain of referrals, disconnected from the first. Limitations included the possible bias of both the participants and the researcher. Biases of participants may have included opinions based on atypical experiences, preconceived beliefs about the interview process, or attitudes about the researcher. Those who agreed to participate also may not have reflected the views of the overall teaching community. Researcher biases are grounded in observations and opinions formed over a 15-year period in working with minority at-risk K-12 students and vulnerable populations such as youth offenders and other prisoners. The researcher also has achieved success in promoting student achievement through the incorporation of elements of hip hop culture into secondary and post secondary education and, therefore, has a strong predisposition toward the efficacy of hip hop culture as pedagogy. Another limitation that affects this study includes concerns about the ability to generalize the results to settings beyond those studied.

Definitions

At-risk students: Those students who are at risk of disengaging from school and not attaining grade-appropriate levels of achievement for one or more reasons, such as membership in an ethnic or racial minority, present academic achievement below grade level, low socioeconomic status, or involvement in the juvenile justice system (Hall, 2007; Payne, 2005; Wlodkowski & Ginsberg, 1995).

Curriculum: A set of courses and their content offered at a college or university, or in a K-12 setting.

Generational poverty: Two or more generations who have lived in situations characterized by insufficient resources of various types (Payne, 2005).

Hip hop culture: A youth-based global culture that incorporates the four elements of the MC, or lyricist, the DJ, graffiti, and break dancing; to these four elements is appended the fifth element of a specific body of knowledge. This culture also is characterized by a distinctive lexicon, fashion and worldview (Chang, 2005; Green, 2008; Hill, 2009).

Hip hop education: Sometimes referred to as Hip Hop Based Education (HHBE) or H2ED, this pedagogy utilizes materials such as rap lyrics as authentic texts for study and as a vehicle for the development of critical teaching and thinking skills. The development of technological and media-based skills is another priority. (Green, 2008; Hill, 2009; Stovall, 2008).

Instructional design: The practice of arranging media and content to maximize teacher effectiveness and student learning.

Mentor: A teacher or other member of the learning community who coaches and assists in the professional development of new teachers (Yates, Pelphrey, & Smith, 2008; Whisnant, Elliott, & Pynchon, 2005).

Millennial students: The generation born between approximately 1985 and 2002; they comprise virtually the entire enrollment in the K-12 education system, as well as the majority of traditional-age students currently enrolled in higher education (Coomes & DeBard, 2004).

Oppositional attitude: A student's disengagement from the formal educational process, accompanied by the refusal to participate in required academic activities (Fisher, 2005; Researcher points to pop culture, 2002).

Pedagogy: The strategies or style of instruction; teaching and assisting students through interaction and activity in the academic and social events of the classroom

Popular culture: A range of contemporary media forms including television, movies, music, video games, and elements of hip hop culture (Coomes & DeBard, 2004).

Preparedness: The state of instructional expertise a teacher brings to the classroom, based on formal instruction and other sources.

Professional development: Instruction and activities intended to augment and improve educator knowledge of content, instruction, and strategies.

Professional Development Schools: Collaborative efforts between schools and colleges of education that address the challenge of preparing and retaining qualified and quality teachers for the urban environment (McKinney, Robinson, & Spooner, 2004).

Teacher preparation programs: Higher education programs of varying duration, usually culminating in a bachelor's degree, in a content area specific to practice; alternative models exist.

Transcultural triangularity: The pedagogical and synergistic integration of three cultures with at least three educational objectives to augment student learning outcomes (Stevenson, et al, 2008).

[W]hen we talk about hip-hop in general, hip-hop is preoccupied with life. You could find a hip-hop song dealing with any subject matter, but the stuff that's being promoted and marketed and the corporations are spending major money on is the decadent stuff, which is mostly about drug use and sex. That's why people get a skewed perspective of hip-hop.

Talib Kweli
On Mainstream Hip-Hop and
Honoring the Old School
National Public Radio
April 25, 2013

CAROL A. O'CONNOR, PHD

3 TEACHER PREPAREDNESS RESEARCH

Throughout the course of American history, the interplay of significant trends and events has provided challenges to the public education system. Although the societal context, the role of faculty, the content of curriculum, and the characteristics of students have changed drastically throughout successive eras, the goals of social mobility and economic opportunity have remained desired outcomes (Cohen, 1998). From the Colonial Era onward, educators and other stakeholders have wrestled with questions of pedagogy and how to best meet the needs of their youthful charges (Cohen, 1998).

For a variety of reasons, however, the goal of equitable education has been elusive and, at times, a cruel hoax. Realities such as race-based school segregation, the inability to persist in school due to economic or other constraints, and a variety of political and social factors have excluded segments of the population. These individuals have been precluded from gaining the knowledge and skills necessary to gain economic self sufficiency, as well as the social and human capital that would facilitate upward mobility (Cabrerra & La Nasa, 2000; Freire, 2007; Hossler, Schmidt, & Vesper, 1999; McDonough, 1997; Morgan, 2002; Payne, 2008).

Topics in this chapter are organized in such a manner as to create a logical flow of ideas. The topic of teacher preparedness is addressed relative to formal and experiential coursework in teacher preparation programs and teachers' subsequent perceptions of their own preparedness. Issues of at-risk students, distressed schools, and curricular issues are presented, as well as an overview of the literature addressing issues of curricular relevance and its role in increasing teacher preparedness and effectiveness. Topics are presented in the following order: teacher preparedness, professional development schools, teachers' perceptions, induction and mentoring programs, urban schools, and at-risk students. It is important to note that the interrelated nature of these elements necessitates recurrent reiterations and references throughout this chapter.

Teacher Preparedness

Research findings consistently indicate that high quality teachers are the major
factor in the achievement of at-risk students (Levine, 2006; Wong & Wong, 2004). Although the factors that produce quality teachers are seemingly open-ended and subject to controversy, Levine (2006) found that a majority of teacher candidates have received their training in university programs characterized by low admission standards and graduation rates. In his study, Levine (2006) identified nine criteria by which teacher-training programs should be evaluated. Some of the features particularly germane to the topics addressed in this investigation include: (a) clearly defined programmatic purpose, aligned with the needs of schools, teachers, and students; (b) curricular coherence, targeted to the needs of teachers at specific types of schools; (c) a balanced approach to instruction that combines theory and practice; and (d) assessment of the program through high-quality research. One of the most significant findings of Levine's (2006) study was the link between the quality of university teacher training and the subsequent achievement of K-12 students.

With these factors in mind, the work of other researchers becomes more relevant to this context of inquiry. One debate that has been prevalent in the educational community regards the content of teacher-training programs. Although research repeatedly points to findings that note the importance of preparing teachers for cultural diversity of all types, and consideration of the sociocultural, linguistic, cognitive, and other critical characteristics of the students with whom teacher candidates will eventually work, school policy remains mired in standards-based notions of student achievement (Weiner, 2000). There is consensus among many researchers regarding the importance for the classroom teacher in urban settings to have knowledge of the factors shaping their students' lives, as well as their interests (Darling-Hammond, & McLaughlin, 2003; Hill, 2009; Kitwana, 2002; Liston, Whitcomb, & Borko, 2006; Weiner, 2000).

Cognizant of the increasing global nature of the economic and social spheres, members of the education community currently are working to make sure teachers have the knowledge and skills they need to ensure that students from challenging backgrounds receive the benefits of an education that is truly equitable (Garcia, 2002; Giallo & Little, 2003; Marbley, Bonner, McKisick, Henfield, & Watts, 2007; Yates, Pelphrey, & Smith, 2008). Unfortunately, some researchers and authors of books widely read in the K-12 teaching community do not address the topic of relevance (Smokler, 2005; Wong, & Wong, 2004) and mention the element of culture only in passing, sometimes in a derogatory manner (Wong, & Wong, 2004).

Professional Development Schools

The attempts to meet the needs of teacher candidates and those whom they will instruct in high-need areas have been a source of consternation. Various proposals have been designed to bridge the gap so that all students have the opportunity for a rigorous and equitable education. At present, professional training programs vary in duration from one to five years (Levine, 2006). Levine (2006) finds that rigorous five-year programs are the most effective, although other successful models exist.

These five-year programs frequently fall into the category of Professional Development Schools. They include a strong component of sustained classroom experience during teacher training (Darling-Hammond, & McLaughlin, 2003; Levine, 2006; McKinney, Robinson, & Spooner, 2004). Professional Development Schools are characterized by a partnership between a higher education teacher preparation program and one or more schools in the public K-12 system (Cherubini, 2006). Teachers involved in these five-year programs often report satisfaction with their experience (Cherubibi, 2006). Although a quantitative study found no significant differences in effective urban teacher characteristics between groups of new teachers who had received their pre-

service training in these schools and those who had attended traditional four-year programs, the researchers acknowledged that the differing procedures, standards, components, and duration made it difficult to compare randomly assigned groups and arrive at conclusions that are reliable and valid (McKinney, Robinson, & Spooner, 2004).

Teacher Perceptions

Many new and veteran teachers report that they are not well prepared to meet the educational needs of diverse learners, especially at-risk urban students. To add clarity to this discussion, some components that teachers feel comprise teaching competence include thorough preparation in both content knowledge and theory, good classroom management skills, and the ability to communicate well with parents and other stakeholders (Huntley, 2008). Oddly, the role of student interaction, relevance in the curriculum, or other student-oriented factors are not mentioned here, although another section states that teachers in this phenomenographic study did report the importance of facilitating student learning (Huntley, 2008).

A mixed-methods study using triangulation of data examined teachers' views of their schools as communities of inquiry. The researcher found that teachers' expectations of professional inquiry were aligned with best practices but noted that many schools did not meet these criteria (Cherubini, 2006; Cherubini, 2008). Cherubini (2008) also pointed out that overall findings of his study were that the teaching practicum experience of study participants had a significantly negative effect on their beliefs about schools acting as professional communities of inquiry to improve teaching and learning. The researcher posited that such disillusionment and dissatisfaction often lead to teacher attrition (Cherubini, 2008).

Urban Schools

Distressed schools in high-poverty urban areas are hampered by inadequate funding, large class size, inadequately prepared students, and low teacher morale (Ahuja, 2007; Foote, 2005; Jacob, 2007; Thompson & Smith, 2005). Many teachers – especially those who work in high-poverty schools – report feeling inadequately prepared to meet the challenges posed by teaching at-risk children (Allen, 2003; NCES, 2001; Weiner, 2000). Teacher turnover rate is high, and young teachers who come into these institutions typically leave within five years or less (Alliance for Excellent Education, 2005; Gonzalez, Brown, & Slate, 2008; Seltzer, 2007).

Formal and informal teacher induction programs and effective interaction with a knowledgeable mentor have shown promise in helping new teachers gain the site-specific knowledge and skills needed to meet student needs. In challenging urban settings, this support may be imperative to increase teaching effectiveness and reduce teacher attrition (Ahuja, 2007; Haberman, 2008; Jacob, 2007). Since many urban schools are struggling to recruit and retain effective teachers (Jacob, 2007), federal government programs such as Teach for America have been implemented to address the need in underserved schools throughout the country. However, most of these first- and second-year teachers came from socioeconomic conditions vastly different from their students (Jacob, 2007; Kozol, 2005; Payne, 2008; Seltzer, 2007). Many of them reported that neither their university pre-service training nor the training undertaken prior to their entry into these settings adequately prepared them for the realities they faced. The most common problem reported by these teachers related to issues of classroom management, and in one report, teachers described the training they had received as virtually useless (Seltzer, 2007).

At-risk Students

Many new teachers are dismayed by the paucity of at-risk students' basic knowledge and academic skills (Kozol, 2005; Payne, 2005; Seltzer, 2007; Thompson & Smith, 2005), as well as their disengagement from the educational process (Bonny, Britto, Klostermann, Hornung, & Slap, 2000; Comissiong, 2007; Researcher points to pop culture, 2000; Wlodkowski & Ginsberg, 1995). Payne (2005) notes that many households where children live in poverty lack adequate space or lighting for completion of homework assignments; such households also may lack books and basic school supplies such as a globe, paper, pencils and folders. Furthermore, parents may be unable to help children with assignments, or even to spend time reading to them, due to demanding work schedules that leave them exhausted, or the fact of their own limited levels of educational attainment.

Poverty presents a set of challenges which may include insufficient financial resources, inadequate access to health care and other services, lack of appropriate role models, or unavailability of child care for working parents (Fass & Cauthen, 2007; Koch, 2007). Constraints such as these may often seem overwhelming, and individuals must muster a range of strategies and resources in order to manage the realities faced on a daily basis (Comissiong, 2007; Dyson, 2007; Freire. 2007; Garcia, 2002; Hill, 2009; Payne, 2005). Frequently living in areas where unemployment is high, and where violence, crime and other dangers to personal safety are more likely to occur, children and adults become preoccupied with survival (McKinney, Robinson, & Spooner, 2004; Payne, 2005). McKinney, Robinson, and Spooner (2004) add that other characteristics of urban districts include achievement gaps between groups, especially between the majority and minority populations, and by high dropout rates. For many people who live in poverty, belief in the efficacy of education often becomes eroded (Payne, 2005).

With the United States public education system under scrutiny from both the public and private sectors and increased levels of concern about student success, it becomes imperative to examine how teachers can best meet the needs of all students. The model of acquiescent students absorbing knowledge and accepting direction from teachers has been shown to be insufficient (Fisher, 2005; Freire 2007; Garcia 2002), and it has become necessary to evaluate and incorporate both content and strategies that fully engage students as partners in their own learning process (Coomes & DeBard, 2004; Green, 2008; Hill, 2009). Many of the characteristics of poverty influence behaviors and attitudes that may not promote academic achievement within the context of the curriculum delivery methods currently taught to pre-service teachers (Fisher, 2005; Levine, 2006). The term oppositional attitude is frequently used to describe these students' disengagement (Fisher, 2005). Several researchers have found that effective teachers must take these characteristics into account when working with at-risk students and they expect that college and university programs would include instruction based on these principles (Hill, 2009; Seltzer, 2007; Stovall, 2008).

Many young people report feeling that school has no relevance to their lives or future plans (Comissiong, 2007; Garcia, 2002). Kagan (1990) asserts that typical school culture transforms at-risk students into a discrete subculture diametrically opposed to academic success. A wide body of literature points to the importance of relevance in the curriculum to maximize student engagement in the learning process (Burke-Adams, 2007; Comissiong, 2007; Dyson, 2007; Freire, 2007; Hill, 2009; Payne, 2005; Stovall, 2006; Stovall, 2008); these authors agree that relevance is central to the teacher's task of actively engaging students, and in the development of their critical thinking skills. Other researchers point to the necessity of addressing students' differing learning styles (Gardner,1993; Payne, 2005), and basing instructional design on the principles of learning discovered through brain research (Smokler, 2005).

Innovative Pedagogies

With the aforementioned research in mind, it is necessary to examine some of the
innovative pedagogies that differ from traditional methods, especially those that have taken center stage in the currently standards-driven educational environment. Environmental factors such as the prevalence of hip hop culture, and the centrality of the encoded and explicit messages contained therein, should be considered when examining pedagogical practices that may boost teacher effectiveness (Dyson, 2007; Garcia, 2002; Gardner, 1993; Ginswright, 2004; Henderson, 2004; Kitwana, 2002; Kitwana, 2005; Levine, 2006; Rose, 1994; Stovall, 2006). Burke-Adams (2004) recommends striking a balance between the demands of standardized accountability and students' needs for creative expression; she points out that creativity is an essential element in the development of problem-solving skills, which have applicability in science and technology, as well as in art. Creativity, the ability to synthesize ideas, and to work in a disciplined manner are considered some of the competencies necessary to thrive in a society characterized by unprecedented change (Gardner, 2006).

Rockwell (2007) researched the efficacy of accessing students' prior knowledge in relationship to concept development and found that such strategies assist at-risk students in overcoming motivational barriers to learning. Hall (2007) interviewed students during the data collection phase of a qualitative study and noted links between low academic achievement of adolescent non-white males and the stresses associated with dealing with the stereotyping of minority cultures, the search for an authentic sense of masculinity, and other factors. He studied a youth outreach program that offered young males the opportunity to express themselves through creative written expression in the form of poetry, spoken word and hip hop, and noted the coping strategies and evidence of resilience revealed in these written texts (Hall, 2007). This finding is consistent with the work of other researchers who have noted students' increased levels of engagement and achievement when elements of verbal creativity are a part of instruction (Duncan-Andrade, & Morrell, 2005; Green, 2008; Hill, 2009; Rose, 1994).

Many researchers and other authors have examined elements of hip hop culture from a variety of perspectives. While some have analyzed the internal elements and explicit messages of rap lyrics (Adams & Fuller, 2007; Green, 2008; Hamilton, 2004; Iwamoto, 2003; Ogbar, 1999; Oware, 2007; Relic, 2007; Sullivan, 2003), others have extended this discussion to the use of hip hop lyrics as a form of pedagogy (Ciccariello-Maher, 2007; Darby & Shelby, 2005; Runnell, 2008; Green, 2008; Harrison, Moore & Evans, 2006; Henderson, 1996).

The prevalence of hip hop culture as a global youth phenomenon is viewed by some scholars as a context within which to engage students and develop the connections between their lived experiences and academic materials. From its origins as a distinct form of artistic expression created more than 30 years ago by disadvantaged black and Latino youth reared in conditions of generational poverty in the Bronx, hip hop has grown in influence to the point that it has a major impact on speech, clothing, behaviors, attitudes, and intellectual perspectives (Chang, 2005; Cushman, 2007; Dyson, 2007; George, 1998; Henderson, 2004; Hill, 2009; Kitwana, 2002; Morgan, 2002; Perry, 2004; Pinderhughes, 1997; Price, 2007; Rose, 1994; Samy, 2007; Smitherman, 2002). Many young people are deeply influenced by media such as television, movies and popular music (Coomes & De Bard, 2004; Hill, 2009; Payne, 2005), and have identified in significant ways with the images and concerns of hip hop culture, especially as they are expressed in the lyrical content of rap music (Chang, 2002; Dyson, 2007; Green, 2008; Hill, 2009; Kitwana, 2002; Kitwana, 2005; Morgan, 2002; Runnell, 2008).

Many researchers state that environmental factors such as the prevalence of hip hop music, and the centrality of the encoded and explicit messages contained therein, should be considered when examining pedagogical practices that may boost teacher effectiveness (Comissiong, 2007; Dyson, 2007; Garcia, 2002; Ginswright, 2004; Henderson, 2004, Kitwana, 2002; Rose, 1994; Thompson & Smith, 2005). Rap lyrics typically tell the stories of people's lives and experiences, and their aspirations and sorrows, but do so in such a frank vernacular that many people have deemed this art form offensive and rejected it as a negative influence on teenagers and young adults (Adams, & Fuller, 2007; Ogbar, 1999; Oware, 2007; Sullivan, 2003). Rose (2008) addresses many of these criticisms and concludes that while some have a measure of validity, others are overgeneralizations that result in an inappropriate rejection of the entire genre. In fact, other researchers have found great value in these texts, and have used them to build critical thinking, oral and written skills in areas as diverse as social justice, language arts, history, mathematics and science (Comissiong, 2007; Green, 2008; Hill, 2009; Runnell, 2008; Stoval, 2006, Stovall, 2008). The effective use of rap lyrics is considered as a possible way to bridge the gaps in teacher preparedness, to deliver academic content, and to enable teachers to better understand and engage diverse learners (Chang, 2002; Ciccariello-Maher, 2007; Green, 2008; Kitwana, 2005; Perry, 2004; Stovall, 2008).

Then the music for you is about building a community.

I don't think that music should be above the people. Class doesn't cost a dime, and you spread it around. Knowledge, wisdom, and understanding don't come out of the microwave. You got to keep moving forward because the evil doesn't stop.

Chuck D
Interview
The Progressive
July 8, 2005

4 DEVELOPING A FRAMEWORK

In addressing the issue of teacher preparedness and the factors that make such preparation effective, the influences of both formal instruction and experiential instruction were examined. Formal instruction includes the pre-service curriculum studied prior to graduation from a four- or five-year program undertaken at a college or university. Formal instruction also includes the training teachers receive in the school where they gain employment; in this context, the role of state and federal laws was considered. Professional development activities include the contribution to learning provided by conferences and workshops that address issues of student behavior, literacy, and pedagogy.

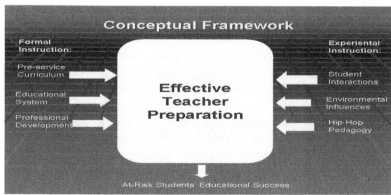

Figure 1. Conceptual Framework

Experiential instruction refers to the type of input teachers receive during the course of their professional activities. From interaction with students, especially those from diverse backgrounds, teachers have the opportunity to develop a deeper understanding of students' circumstances, perspectives, and concerns. Environmental influences include the role of generational poverty, as well as factors such as the pervasiveness of the media and hip hop culture, and the impact of these on students' identity formation, attitudes and perceptions (Chang, 2005; Coomes & DeBard, 2004; Kitwana, 2005).

As discussed above, these elements are of importance since they provide a meaningful framework within which the investigations undertaken in this study were structured. By first examining the role and impact of formal teacher training programs and subsequent professional development activities, it became clear that success in utilizing this information to facilitate student engagement and achievement was not the usual outcome (Darling-Hammond & McLaughlin, 2003; Freire, 2007; Giallo & Little, 2003; Levine, 2006). The growing emphasis on student-centered pedagogy precipitated a thorough examination of the characteristics of millennial students, especially at-risk urban youth (Hill, 2009; Payne, 2005; Stovall, 2006; Stovall, 2008). Since the literature suggests that student engagement and achievement are increased through the inclusion of rap music or other elements of hip hop culture, special attention was focused on the role of this innovative pedagogy (Dyson, 2007; Green, 2008, Hill, 2009; Stovall, 2006).

The exploration of factors involved in effective teacher training was undertaken as a qualitative study. Initial understanding of what constitutes and produces effectiveness in teacher training activities was gained through examination of the relevant literature, and it was expected that, in the data collection phase, comprehension would be augmented as meanings emerged during interactions with participants. It should be noted that during the course of interviews, new directions were illuminated that created opportunities for the researcher to examine the literature in those areas as well. In particular, the emphasis participants placed on the importance of hip hop to their students, and the teachers' self-perceived success in using this pedagogy to augment student engagement and achievement, motivated the researcher to delve more deeply into the research on this topic. A phenomenological approach was utilized throughout. Research questions addressed the curricular content of teacher-training programs in relation to the academic needs of at-risk students and investigated innovative programs and practices that promote teacher preparedness. The interview guide allowed for a variety of responses, as well as accommodation of new topics as introduced by the respondents. Research questions are as follows:

1. How does formal teacher training prepare teachers to meet students' needs?

2. How does experiential training affect teacher preparedness?

3. How do the characteristics of students from diverse background impact teacher
   preparedness?

4. What recommendations do teachers propose to inform practice and enhance
   preparedness?

Rationale for Research Design/Methodology

A qualitative methodology best suited exploration of the topic of teacher
preparedness since it enabled participants to be more introspective and reflective, to fully express their views and opinions, and to tell their stories (Creswell, 2003; Johnson, 2006). Methodological features of this paradigm take into account the intersecting effects that take place in social settings (Denzin & Lincoln, 2005; Hoepfl, 1997). It also allowed for recognition of the value-laden nature of inquiry, as well as the socially constructed nature of reality (Denzin & Lincoln, 2000; Denzin & Lincoln, 2003). The topic of effective teacher preparedness is multifaceted and required the application of linguistic analysis to best explain the content, meaning, and significance of the data. A narrative research design was well suited to this study in that it enabled the researcher to describe fully both the context and content of the interview data. It was expected that interviewees' responses would create opportunities to delve into new and unexpected areas of inquiry that would serve to illuminate and enrich the data (Cresswell, 1998; Denzin & Lincoln, 2000; Lincoln

& Guba, 1985). In-person and telephone interviews were digitally recorded and then transcribed. Field notes were taken and a research journal kept to enhance the understanding of content within context.

Assumptions and Biases

Assumptions included those pertaining to the contributions of the participants during interviews. For example, it was assumed that participants were truthful, that they were knowledgeable, that they had ample time to reply in depth to inquiries, and that they had the willingness to do so. It also was assumed that their input would be of value to the study. Further assumptions were that sites selected for this study were representative, and that the resultant findings would add to the national discussion. Another assumption that affected this study included concerns about the ability to generalize the results to settings beyond those studied.

Biases included those of the researcher and participants. It is acknowledged that the researcher is a socially situated being, with a distinct history and set of beliefs. (Denzin & Lincoln, 2003). Researcher biases are grounded in observations and opinions formed over a 15-year period in working with at-risk students and vulnerable populations such as prisoners. The researcher also has achieved success in promoting student engagement and achievement through the incorporation of elements of hip hop culture into secondary and postsecondary education and, therefore, has a strong predisposition toward the efficacy of hip hop culture as pedagogy. Other researcher biases included the tendency to seek out members of the hip hop community who are or were teachers, and to interview individuals who were open to the use of or experimentation with this, or other, innovative forms of pedagogy. To help offset the effects of these biases, the researcher kept an interview journal to note participants' reactions, emotions and non-verbal cues.

Biases of participants included opinions based on experiences that may not be typical of those experienced by others in their category, preconceived beliefs about the interview process, or attitudes about the researcher. Those who agreed to participate also may not have reflected the views of the overall educational community. Interviewee biases might have included those either similar to the researcher's or ones that stand in contrast to these views. To overcome the possible effects of these biases, the researcher was careful to include a variety of interviewees and to utilize the services of a peer debriefer.

Site Selection

Sites for data collection were purposefully selected and determined on the basis of factors such as appropriateness to the nature of the study, appropriateness to the nature of this doctoral program, availability of study participants and accessibility (Cresswell, 2003). With these considerations in mind, the researcher focused primarily on the selection of sites located in urban areas, especially those that serve high numbers of at-risk students. Since hip hop has its origins in the high-poverty areas of New York City, similar urban areas with high numbers of poor, minority students were chosen. A brief description of each of the locations is provided to further elucidate the reasons for their selection. As was expected, interviews took place in classrooms, offices and other sites on the campuses or at other locations convenient for study participants; three of the interviews were conducted on the telephone. Access to physical sites was gained through requests to the district's director for research and accountability or other gatekeepers.

Participant Selection

Participants were selected through the judicious use of snowball qualitative sampling. This technique is a form of purposive sampling in which participants are asked to recommend other individuals as participants (Creswell, 2003; Marshall, 1998; Qualitative Research Methods, n.d.). Creswell (2003) states that this process typically proceeds after the study begins and adds that referrals may be gleamed during the interview process or through informal conversations. This technique has the advantage of allowing for flexibility and modification as new topics and themes emerge from the data (Qualitative Research Methods, n.d.).

While snowball sampling ideally provides a smoothly linked chain of referrals, several researchers have warned of the potential problems inherent in this model. Biernacki and Waldorf (1981)

CAROL A. O'CONNOR, PHD

state that specific problem areas include finding respondents to start the referral chains, controlling the types of chains and number of participants in each chain, and the pacing and monitoring of the chains. Another significant concern with this model is the monitoring of data quality. Since participants are not randomly selected, snowball sampling is subject to numerous biases (Denzin & Lincoln, 2000; Marshall, 1998).

During this study the flexibility of snowball sampling allowed for the recruitment of teachers drawn from a network of individuals who offered fresh and sometimes unexpected ideas and insights. Shifts in the direction of participant recruitment occurred several times during the research process, however. New chains, some with only one or two links, were created during this process as needed.

Attempts were made to include working teachers at different grade levels who felt they had exhibited success in the classroom, as well as those who reported that they began their teaching career under-prepared for the realities they faced. To gain a wider perspective, some teachers who entered the profession through alternative routes also were selected for interviews, as well as one former teacher known for his incisive intellect and strong viewpoints. A total of 11 interviews were conducted. This number was deemed sufficient for the purposes of this study; in addition to the practical consideration of time and deadline constraints, the data were saturated since all participants offered comments and suggestions that arrived at similar conclusions.

Initial contact with the intended participants was made through personal introductions to the researcher or telephone calls facilitated by referrals from teachers and other individuals; formal letters were distributed requesting permission from the intended participants followed. Accurate and complete records of all calls that were made, letters, or other forms of correspondence were kept. Appropriate permission from the Institutional Review Board of the researcher's university was obtained and documented. Other items include the letter of request to conduct research, the letter of approval to conduct research, the letter of invitation, consent to participate in research form, permission to audio record the interview form, and the interview guide. A personal profile is also included.

Interview Guide

Participants were asked to respond to a few closed-ended questions in order to produce factual information but the primary focus was on a series of loosely structured, open-ended questions designed to elicit their individual views, experiences and perspectives. These prompts asked teachers to describe the content of their pre-service training and to expound upon the effectiveness of this body of knowledge in the classroom. Teachers also had the opportunity to describe their students, explain salient features of what they have learned on the job, and how effective they felt in working with at-risk students. Those who felt they were not adequately prepared were asked to comment on what they thought would have better prepared them to meet these students' needs. However, since the majority of participants had not participated in a formal pre-service training program, the emphasis in interviews with these individuals centered around the teaching strategies they felt were most effective with students.

Data Collection Procedures

The researcher conducted interviews in person and occasionally by telephone with participants. Each interview consisted of closed-ended, as well as open-ended questions. A particular benefit of closed ended questions was that they allowed the researcher to obtain information supportive of the literature. Open ended questions, on the other hand, allowed for a deep investigation into the central questions of the study. Consent to participate in the study and to have an audio recording made was obtained prior to initiation of the interview process. Interviewee responses were recorded, transcribed, and the data were stored in an electronic file for analysis. Field notes and a research journal were used to supplement data.

Data Analysis

The literature suggests that no clear lines can be drawn to distinguish analysis from the two related components of description and interpretation in a qualitative study (Wolcott, 1994). However, analysis included a carefully documented, systematic, cautious examination of the data, grounded in inherent conservatism (Wolcott, 1994). Through this process, the researcher attempted to capture recurring patterns and note dominant themes throughout the data, leading to the generation of a theory. Wolcott (1994) describes this process as transforming the qualitative data. Other strategies involved in a thorough analysis included a systematic reporting of fieldwork procedures, evaluation of findings, and even a critique of the research process itself. In addition, graphic presentation has been used where it is appropriate.

Trustworthiness

The researcher worked to meet the four criteria identified by Guba and Lincoln (1981) as elements contributing to enhancement of the trustworthiness of the research project. These criteria include credibility, transferability, dependability and confirmability. The literature supports the assertion that taken together with the empirical procedures outlined above; these elements are considered adequate confirmation of the trustworthiness of naturalistic approaches (Lincoln & Guba, 1985). Cresswell (2003) suggests eight primary strategies to promote perceptions of trustworthiness. The more commonly used strategies include triangulation of data sources, member-checking to ascertain accuracy, clarification of researcher bias, and the inclusion of negative or discrepant information. In this investigation, the researcher utilized three of these four strategies; the scope of the study precluded the use of triangulation of data.

Lincoln and Guba (1985) discussed member-checking as a strategy specifically aligned with the element of credibility. They noted that "the task is to obtain confirmation that the report has captured the data as constructed by the informants, or to correct, amend, or extend it" (p. 236). To address the issue of transferability Lincoln and Guba (1985) recommended the use of a rich, descriptive narrative to reveal an accurate picture of the phenomenon under investigation. An in-depth, detailed description of the context of the fieldwork that may allow for transferability is provided in Chapter 4. From this description it is hoped that the reader will be able to decide whether the prevailing environment is representative and whether justification exists for the application of findings to other settings (Shenton, 2004). With a qualitative paradigm, however, the best the researcher can aim for is a limited generalizabilty (Lincoln & Guba, 1985). Dependability was supported through the employment of a dependability audit to assess consistency, accuracy, and predictability among the data (Lincoln & Guba, 1985). Although it is considered difficult to guarantee dependability, the researcher has described the changing context and circumstances that are particular to qualitative research, thereby enabling other researchers to repeat or replicate the investigation (Altheide & Johnson, 1994). In order to achieve confirmability, the researcher has attempted to demonstrate that findings emerged from the data and not from personal predispositions, opinions, views or biases. To support this aim, the researcher kept a reflexive journal. Other methods to ensure confirmability included examination of multiple sources of data, and the use of multiple methods to corroborate the emerging findings.

Factors used to delimit or narrow the scope of this study included focus on the central phenomenon of effective teacher training, focus on efficacy of instruction for at-risk students, selection of specific types and numbers of participants, and the method of naturalistic inquiry planned for data collection. It is possible that the selection of other participants in different locations would have altered the data, leading to different findings.

Inherent in the design of the study itself was the limitation of non-generalizability of findings. Although it is possible that applicability to some settings may be inferred, it is likely that findings might not be useful or appropriate with teachers and students in many others. In addition, it is possible that the findings could be subject to interpretations other than those deduced by the researcher.

45

CAROL A. O'CONNOR, PHD

Excellence is being able to perform at a high level over and over again. You can hit a half-court shot once. That's just the luck of the draw. If you consistently do it... that's excellence.

Jay-Z
Interview
Oprah's Master Class
2015

CAROL A. O'CONNOR, PHD

5 SHAKESPEARE AND JAY-Z

The main research question posed in this study was: How does formal teacher training prepare teachers to meet students' needs? The following three secondary questions relating to student characteristics and how best to guide their learning also were asked: How does experiential training affect teacher preparedness? How do the characteristics of students from diverse backgrounds impact teacher preparedness? What recommendations do teachers propose to inform practice and enhance preparedness?

This chapter presents the results of research regarding the reported sense of preparedness among graduates of teacher-training programs, and teachers who had not had this training, as well as insights they gleaned from actual classroom experience. The findings are presented in three sections. Section one discusses the setting and demographics of the communities in which the participants work. Section two describes the teachers who participated in this study; a pseudonym for each participant was used throughout to protect his or her anonymity. Section 3 evaluates and analyzes the data, and sets the stage for subsequent discussions.

Description of Sites

Since one focus of this study was on the needs of minority urban youth, the researcher was drawn to locations and sites where these students were richly represented. These sites are described in general terms since permission to identify specific schools and districts was not obtained. The two Southern cities are relatively small, with populations less than 300,000; the Southwestern metropolis has a population in excess of 3.5 million. Most of the students in this context were African American, as were all but two of the teachers interviewed. One district had a majority Latino student body.

Since most of the participants were situated in central Mississippi, details about its economy, education system and various social factors are relevant. Mississippi is unique in that it has the only state capital in the United States with a majority black population. Approximately 70.6% of the residents are black, and 27.5% are white, with other races sparsely represented (U.S. Census Bureau, 2008). In 2000 the population of this central city approached 200,000, but by July 2007 this figure had decreased by more than 3% (U.S. Census Bureau, 2008). Recent data show that this city has a higher poverty rate than other portions of the state, with poverty levels among children younger than 18 comprising a disproportionate number of poor residents, nearly double the U.S. average (Mississippi: Demographics and the economy, 2008). In 2007, 45% of the children in the targeted city were living below the poverty level compared with approximately 29% state-wide, and the poverty rate for 12-to-14-year-old males stood at 57% (Mississippi poverty rate data, 2008). The poverty rate for black people of all ages in this area approaches 44%, compared with 16% for white residents (Mississippi: Demographics and the economy, 2008). These conditions are further exacerbated by persistently high rates of unemployment, incarceration, and school dropout behaviors which impact median household figures; non-workers comprise 24% of the population compared to 19% nationwide (Mississippi: Demographics and the economy, 2008).

With an enrollment of 32,000 students, the major school district is the second largest – and only urban – district in the state. The district houses 59 schools: 8 high schools, a career development center, 10 middle schools, 38 elementary schools and two special schools (Mississippi Department of Education, 2009). Most of the participants in this study were working at a high school or elementary school in this district.

The high school had an enrollment of 971 students during the 2006-07 school year, and 1,021 students during the 2008-09 school year. Fifty-one percent of these students were female and 49 % male; enrollment was 100 % African American (Mississippi Department of Education, 2009). The school's website mentions that it is known for the excellence of its boys' basketball team, which has won state titles and other awards (Mississippi Department of Education, 2009). Visitors to the school are welcomed warmly, and requested information and directions willingly given. The grounds are attractively landscaped and well maintained, and the building appears clean and in good repair. No refuse or damage to the physical plant was noted. Students seemed cheerful and pleasant as they transitioned between classes, and they moved about in an orderly fashion. The school utilizes an A/B block schedule that enables students to take eight classes per year and to graduate at least one semester early (Mississippi Department of Education, 2009). One of the two elementary schools serves students in kindergarten through 5th grade and had an enrollment of 580 students during the 2008-09 school year. Black students comprise 96 % of the total enrollment; white students make up about 3 % of enrollment, and Latino students approximately 1%. About 83% of the students qualify for the free or reduced lunch program (Mississippi Department of Education, 2009). Some of the information provided on the school's website is suspect, particularly information about housing unit vacancy in the area; the site sets the vacancy rate figure at 10 %, but a drive through the surrounding area indicates that this figure is probably quite low. The figure for single parent households may not be accurate, since at 22.3 % it seems low, and the same percentage is reported by several other schools in the district. The researcher did not have an opportunity to view the inside of the school since the participant employed there was interviewed in another location.

The other elementary school had 311 pre-kindergarten through 5th grade students during the 2008-09 school year. The school reports a single-parent household rate of 22.3 %, the exact figure reported by some other district schools. The vacancy rate of nearby housing units stood at 18 %, twice the state average. Four classes of each grade level are offered plus four classes for exceptional (Mississippi Department of Education, 2009). The interior of this school evidenced some wear, although staff were friendly and helpful, which constituted an important contribution to the impressions of school climate.

The after-school program is located in a renovated historic home on a quiet side street in a rural community. The interior is spacious and well appointed, with computers and other equipment located in different rooms for individualized work and group projects. Several students were working on wireless laptops, and displayed proficiency in their use of these. About 40 students were enrolled in the program, which was designed to support students with challenges such as low reading levels or involvement with the juvenile justice system. Approximately 12 students attend each day, although different individuals keep the mix in flux. All the students are African American, the majority of them boys. Outside mentors and adults expert in chorus, hip hop, filmmaking and other arts-related activities frequently visit the center to work with students.

With a population of 4,400 this community seemed to differ from the urban areas represented elsewhere in this study. The area's school district has no website, but another source revealed that the district has 4 elementary schools, 2 middle schools and 2 high schools. In 2009 the high school had an enrollment of 524 students, 97% of them black. In 2007 the school did not make Adequate Yearly Progress and was marked for state takeover as a failing school. Despite its idyllic setting, the community faces significant problems with youth gangs, crime, drugs, violence, high dropout rates and other conditions that plague urban centers (Mississippi Department of Education, 2009).

The out-of-state Southern site was located in Louisiana's largest school district, which has 30 elementary schools, 30 middle schools and 22 high schools; there are also four charter schools and 30 private schools within district boundaries (Louisiana Department of Education, 2009). Enrollment for the district's schools is about 45,000 in pre-kindergarten through grade 12. Student demographics district-wide are 76 % black, 20 % white, and 2 % each Hispanic and Asian (Louisiana Department of Education, 2009). From 1989 to 2007 the percentage of white students decreased from 44 % to

20 %, while the percentage of African American students increased from 54 % to 76 % (Louisiana Department of Education, 2009). The participant working in a middle school there was interviewed by phone. He reported that his school has an almost entirely African American student enrollment and that classroom management issues were a particular challenge for many teachers,

especially those who are relatively new to the profession. He said that the school looks clean and well maintained. Most middle schools in the district have a population of about 500 to 550 students (Louisiana Department of Education, 2009).

Two study participants were working in one of the three urban school districts in a major Southwestern city, which taken together house 325 public schools, plus more than 200 charter and private schools (Arizona Department of Education, 2009). One district covers a 220-square-mile area and is fed by 13 elementary schools, making it one of the largest secondary school districts in the nation. A large high school there has more than 70 first languages represented, and more than half the 26,000 students come from homes where English is not the first language (Arizona Department of Education, 2009). Other schools in the area share characteristics of multiple first languages among students, Latino students in excess of 75% of total enrollment, and a large concentration of African American students (Arizona Department of Education, 2009). One participant's school is located in the central portion of a major city; he stated that nearly all of his students are Latinos, many of whom have gang affiliations and other challenges that may interfere with successful school completion. The other participant teaches high school language arts at a school with a high enrollment of Native American students due to its location near an urban reservation. She stated that the school, while clean and otherwise well maintained, has major areas covered with graffiti representing gang affiliations.

All interviews were scheduled at times and places convenient for participants. Six of the interviews took place in the teacher's school of employment; four interviews were conducted via telephone; and one interview took place in the researcher's home. The interviews conducted at the schools allowed for observation of the educational setting and for glimpses into the interactions between teachers and students. Several interviews took place at a high school in central Mississippi, some at an elementary school in another part of that same city, and one at an after-school learning center in a rural area. During the telephone interviews, two interviewees participated from their homes, one took place while the participant was driving en route to an engagement, and the other while the participant was at an undetermined spot in another major southern city. Despite the potential for distraction posed by driving – or in the case of one interviewee, interruptions from other persons in his vicinity – the participants answered questions fully, and the researcher felt confident in the thoroughness and accuracy of the interview data.

The Participants

It is important to note that the sample population was not randomly selected but was collected through a snowball sampling technique. As indicated in Chapter 3, the researcher had a tendency to seek out and obtain referrals from members of the hip hop community. This may account for the fact that three active teachers and one former teacher are rap artists; however, it should be remembered that the other seven teachers, several of whom were older veteran teachers, also provided data that paralleled with that provided by the first group. Of the 11 participants interviewed, six were men and five were women. All were African American except for two white women. Participants' ages ranged from early 20s to mid-50s, although most were younger than 35 years of age; educational attainments varied from pre-bachelor's degree to Ph.D. Since a snowballing technique was used to locate participants, a range of teaching levels and content areas was accessed. Most participants were working in urban schools; the exception was a teacher working in a rural community about 40 minutes drive from a much larger city. The one former teacher interviewed for this study had been working in urban schools before his growing fame pulled him away from the teaching profession.

All participants were assigned pseudonyms and these are used throughout the remainder of this study. Each participant signed two consent forms: one to participate in the study, and the other to allow permission to record the interview. The first participant in this study was assigned the pseudonym Adam. He is a 23-year-old African American who has been teaching creative writing through a grant-based program at an elementary school in South Jackson. Adam was located through an informal conversation, and he verbally agreed to participate in this study. Although he has not undertaken a formal teacher training program, he is considered a gifted rap artist whose lyrics are original, complex and multi-faceted. Adam's lyrics frequently address issues of social justice, the realities of the business world, and the importance of paying attention to the layers of meaning contained within the rhymes. With a youthful appearance and long dreadlocks he looks closer in age and style to many of his students than do many of the other teachers in his school, a fact, he said, that helps students better relate to him.

Barbara, on the other hand, is a seasoned African American teacher in her 34th year of teaching. She presently works with special needs students at a high school in North Jackson. The interview took place in her classroom, initially while her nine students were in music class, but continued upon their return. A full-time assistant works with the class as well, enabling Barbara to direct her attention elsewhere. Although she at first seemed somewhat hesitant to participate in this study, she quickly warmed to her topic and made substantial contributions to the body of data. Barbara demonstrated knowledge of her students by presenting them with individualized assignments geared to their level and interests; she exhibited a control of her classroom that seemed effortless. While the students displayed curiosity about the researcher, they remained quiet and on-task throughout the proceedings, only speaking when the teacher asked for their comments and opinions about the interview questions. Her classroom was clean and orderly, with colorful decorations providing visual interest.

Charles is an African American man who resides in a large Southwestern city, where he has been a 5th-grade mathematics teacher for 7 years. Charles grew up in a Midwestern urban city under very difficult conditions that included birth to a 13-year-old mother who died when Charles was a teenager, a perennially incarcerated father, gang membership, and the death of many of his friends. As a child, he was subjected to physical, emotional, sexual and substance abuse; he reported that as a preschooler, babysitters frequently blew marijuana smoke in his face and laughed when he became disoriented. After a particularly harrowing experience during his teens, he realized that he was not a product of his environment, as he had been told at home and in school, but rather a product of his choices. As a hip hop recording artist he transmits this message of personal responsibility for choices despite one's circumstances.

An African American man in his 20s, Derek has been a full-time teacher for the past one-and-a half years, while concurrently enrolled in an alternative certification program. At the time of the interview he was completing the two-year program and expected to have his own classroom by the start of the 2009-2010 school year. Derek teaches middle school mathematics. Although he holds a degree in marketing, he says his desire to "make a difference in the lives of young people" attracted him to the profession. In addition to his role as a teacher, Derek is also a rap artist whose music ranges from political to spiritual, and includes themes such as love, professions, and other aspects of life. Several of his videos are available on You Tube, a fact that, he says, increases his students' respect for him. Derek was interviewed by telephone. Subsequent to the interview, the researcher watched several of his music videos on You Tube to gain insight into how students might relate to his music.

Prior to her current position as executive director of an after school academic program, Elaine taught at a community college for 10 years. She holds a Ph.D. in psychology and since 2005 has directed a program that serves students attending school under court order, gang members, other students in danger of dropping out of school, and occasionally a few students who are no longer enrolled in school. A middle-aged white woman with blond hair and bright blue eyes, she spoke respectfully of her students and evidenced interest in their ideas and preferences. She discussed their talents, as well as the academic limitations that may retard their progress through the educational pipeline. She said, for example, that some students entered the after-school program with 2nd-grade reading skills, some are working toward a GED, and several others attend because they perceive it to be a safe place where they gain temporary shelter from the harsh realities of their lives. Elaine tutors students in mathematics and language arts, and oversees their media-based activities. She presented a perspective on what best meets students' needs, and offered evidence to back her assertions.

Florence is an African American woman in her late 20s who has been teaching for seven years at an elementary school in central Jackson. The school is visibly less affluent than the others visited, but the atmosphere was friendly and calm, even at the end of a school day a week before summer vacation. The older building was clean and well maintained, and sunlight streamed into the hallways through long rows of large windows. A native of Jackson, Florence radiated an air of cheerful confidence and spoke with assurance about her perceptions of effective teaching. She discussed her 5th-grade students and her strategies for working with them that have resulted in their engagement and measured gains in learning.

After pursuing other professions, Gwen entered the field of education through an alternative certification route. Currently enrolled in a master's degree program, she has been teaching while working toward full certification. Gwen is an African American woman in her early 40s who exudes an air of quiet confidence. She currently teaches 5th grade at an elementary school in the mid-city area of Jackson.

Helen is an African American woman approximately 45 years of age. Although she completed both her bachelor's and master's degrees in the field of education, she is another of the study participants who pursued certification through an alternative program. At the time of this interview she had just completed her 6th year of teaching in a mid-city elementary school.

Iris is a white woman who works at a large high school in Phoenix that contains a diverse student population of Latino and Native American students, as well as smaller numbers of blacks, whites and Asians. She has a master's degree in education, but did not seek certification until she began teaching high school in the mid-1990s. Now in her mid- to late 50s, she just completed her 15th year of teaching; she has been at her current school for 8 years.

A teacher who participated in a formal teacher training program, James has been working at the same high school for 10 years. A slim, youthful African American man in his early 30s, he teaches mathematics and is assistant band director. While attending to after-school activities with a group of students, James clearly explained the relationship between his formal and experiential learning.

Kenneth is the pseudonym assigned to an internationally famous rap artist who had worked as a substitute teacher in settings more varied than those reported by any of the other participants. Although all of the schools he was assigned to are in urban areas, he worked with students ranging from kindergarten through 12th grade, and taught subjects ranging from mathematics to language

arts. In addition to his music career, he is
well-known as a hip hop activist who especially champions the
educational rights of minority youth; some of his lyrics address this
topic directly.

Analysis of Findings

Upon completion of the interviews, the data were transcribed
and researcher's notes were appended to the transcripts. The
transcripts were carefully examined for word frequency and
conversation analysis as outlined by Denzin and Lincoln (2003).
Words and sentences were examined for content and context, and
meanings were cautiously interpreted. Transcripts were analyzed
line by line and compared with all other transcripts one by one. As
a result of this analysis it became possible to accurately compare
the responses to each of the interview questions. The eight major
questions asked during the each of the interviews and an
interpretative examination of participants' responses follows. It is
important to note that participants' responses to specific questions
often included responses to other questions as well. For this
reason, quotations drawn from the data have been organized and
reported in a manner designed to facilitate a flow of ideas
congruent with the literature.

After initial questions were posed to elicit teachers' background
information, they were asked to describe the content and process
of their pre-service teacher training. There was a variety of answers
since some participants had participated in traditional teacher
preparation programs while others had chosen an alternative route
to certification. Those who were enrolled in four-year university
programs stated that their course work included psychology,
behavioral management, classroom management, reading
fundamentals, theories of reading, public law, curriculum and
instruction, and courses designed to acquaint them with the
challenges inherent in meeting the needs of exceptional students.
Course work for intended high school teachers also included focus
on a specific content area, as well as the skills necessary to teach
content. Frequent or occasional observations also were part of
these formal programs. One participant described the field
observations as "just looking and you sit in the classroom maybe
90 minutes for maybe twice a week for maybe six to seven weeks.

All you are is a fly on the wall."

An area that prompted a wide variety of responses was the nature of the practicum. Also referred to as the internship, or more simply as student teaching, respondents reported that their practicum varied in length from two eight-week sessions, or basically one semester, to as little as a few weeks. During this period of internship, actual teaching time varied as well; James stated that his student teaching took place at two different schools, with one cooperating teacher being a great deal more supportive and giving him an opportunity to actually gain experience teaching, while the other "had a rough time letting go and letting me really take the reins." The amount and quality of feedback provided by cooperating teachers also varied widely. James stated that one of his cooperating teachers "wanted to jump in and give open critiques in front of the students about what she thought I should be doing." Other teachers noted that their cooperating teachers gave them no feedback at all. Florence reported that her practicum was

. . . a very, very short time. I was just petty much observing. I wasn't teaching and the chance that I did get to teach, it was just one time. She just let us take over for that day and just get a feel of what she was doing in the classroom. But it really wasn't my class or my students; it wasn't being able to take over for a whole six months, or a whole week for that matter.

Due to a persistent teacher shortage in critical areas, and to the midlife career change patterns currently prevalent nationwide, alternative programs have been designed to facilitate teacher certification within a relatively short period of time. These programs appeal to younger people as well, especially those who have already obtained a bachelor's degree in some other field. Most of the alternative programs in which study participants have participated in are of a two-year duration. After graduating from university with a degree in marketing, Derek decided to work in education. "I really had a desire to be in a profession where I could make a difference in the lives of young people, so I wanted to be a teacher," he said.

Derek began teaching middle school mathematics immediately

CAROL A. O'CONNOR, PHD

after earning his bachelor's degree, and at the time of this interview he was still enrolled in the alternative program. His coursework has included subjects such as classroom management, different learning styles and how to work with special needs students. Program content also has included focus on student behaviors based on socioeconomic factors. "Like they are dealing with parents who are absent or in jail," he explained. The program is self-paced and students must pass a test to obtain certification.

Both Helen and Gwen have undertaken alternative programs prior to certification. Helen's program consisted of 32 credit hours of coursework which included classroom management, statistics and a class in exceptional education. Gwen began her work toward certification after she was already employed as a teacher under an emergency license. In addition to courses in classroom management and testing measurements, she completed the Praxis 1 and Praxis 2 tests which demonstrate proficiency in reading and mathematics and in one's chosen content area. Gwen credits her school district for providing instructional support that helped her master the content needed for passing Praxis 1. "We went every Saturday for four weeks and they gave us a practice book," she said. Five observations of her teaching also were part of the program. Helen and Gwen work at the same elementary school and both said they know other teachers there who are pursuing an alternative route to certification.

Interestingly, not one participant reported that the pre-service teacher training they had undertaken fully equipped them to meet the challenges faced in classrooms of their own. Among those who graduated from a traditional preparation program, the perceptions of program effectiveness varied. Barbara gave her program the best grade. "I think it gave me a good insight on what to do in a regular classroom," she said, and added that "maybe about three-fourths helped me." James also viewed his pre-service training in a positive light and stated that it was "as adequate as it could be for teachers. I always tell people, education is only going to be 60% of it."

Other teachers were less sanguine. Charles reported that "at the university we had great discussions," but that legislators and some school administrators "have no understanding of what's going on in the classroom, what type of students we're trying to educate." He added that the university training he received "doesn't help us

60

to deal with our students, the type of students we're dealing with today." Florence felt that her training

> . . . really wasn't helpful. I would say it helped very little due to the fact that it was based more on terminology rather than just the teaching approach. They wanted you to know what this meant, what this term meant in relation to the children, rather than what we're supposed to do with the children once we get them. They told us the different behaviors to look for, but not actually how to deal with the behaviors. So I would say that it really wasn't helpful.

Kenneth's responded in a similar vein.

> Did the training help me? Nah, I don't think so. What happens is, the problems that are in our communities and our classrooms are so big that it's going to take something big in order to combat it. If you look at statistics and look at the dropout rates of kids, it's going to take something revolutionary and unconventional to bring these kids back.

Teachers who gained certification or who were working on certification through an alternative program also had mixed feelings about their preparation programs. Derek said his training has "helped to a degree, but honestly, on-the-job experience is the best teacher. Definitely it helps, but you have to confront the problems you hear about in class." Helen concurred with Derek's assessment and stated she felt the training "helped a little bit. As far as someone going to get the actual training, that's great. But as far as having that hands-on experience, that's the best."

Three participants – Adam, Iris and Elaine – had no formal pre-service teacher training at all. Iris was able to gain teacher certification in Arizona through a waiver, since she had taught at a community college for three years; also, classes she took in a master's level course in second language acquisition were counted as English courses in Arizona, thereby giving her enough credits to merit a content-area certification. She admitted that her first year in the high school classroom was especially difficult since she had had no training in classroom management. "As far as instruction I think I was ok, but the kids acted really badly and I had no idea how to prevent that. At first they were ok, but once things got out of hand, I didn't know how to gain control." Gwen stated that the master's program she was currently enrolled in has proved helpful in several areas:

> I have been able to take at least one thing from each of those classes. It's giving me a lot of the tools and resources that I didn't have. It's teaching me how to teach reading, teaching me about different learning styles, interventions, just everything you'll need in the classroom.

Adam exhibited a resiliency and sense of self-direction that he felt accounted for a portion of his success with students. "I don't know if it's because of my age, or because I'm a male, or because I talk to them differently, but a lot of the behavioral problems that their normal teachers have, I don't have," he said. He added that he had basically trained himself how to deliver lessons that effectively engage students.

As indicated in the review of literature, mentoring or other support provided by the school may increase teacher preparedness. Mentoring may be formal or informal; the school or district may assign a seasoned teacher in the same grade level or content area to new teachers for a period of 1 or 2 years. James stated that he had had a form of mentoring as an undergraduate student that provided assistance in studying for the state certification examination. After graduation, however, no formal university plan existed to follow his development or to help ease him into full-time classroom work. Barbara reported a similar experience. She said that she had no mentoring provided either by the district or her school when she started teaching. "At that time it was just you graduate and you're done," she noted. James added that "Back then they didn't have an outreach program where they'd come back and check on me, but this school itself had something set up." He said that new teachers were paired with a senior teacher in the same content area: "I could meet with them at the end of the day, or they would definitely come to find me every two weeks or so to ask how things were going, and where was my head, and things like that." His school also provided an array of training seminars that covered issues ranging from classroom management to stress management and health maintenance. "If you don't pay attention to your health and how you manage stress, you can drive yourself into the ground," he added.

Florence said that she had a mentor assigned to her during her first two years as a teacher who supported her by answering questions about instruction and student behavior issues, and helping with the acquisition of outside resources. Although Florence found this help of genuine benefit, she added that, "I think she's been teaching like for 40-something years, so being she's a veteran teacher, she has a lot of things that are not up-to-date with the kids we have now." Helen said her mentor worked with her for a year.

> That person just came into the classroom to make sure you
> have it organized, help you with bulletin boards, and hanging
> up stuff on the front of your door, but she wasn't a mentor
> as far as someone assisting me with writing lesson plans
> and that type of thing.

Iris added that she got very little help from the school during her induction phase. "The principal showed me where my room was and gave me the book, and basically just said, 'Good luck.' I didn't even know what I was supposed to teach, or even where the restroom was." A senior English teacher was assigned to her as a mentor, although actual assistance was minimal. "She told me to come see her if I had any questions, but I had so many I didn't even know where to start," Iris recalled ruefully. "So I rarely went to see her, and she rarely checked on me."

Several teachers reported benefit from participation in professional development activities. Florence stated that

> Most of the workshops we go through help with incentives,
> what we need to do in the classroom, some things that might
> help with our students. I can honestly say I have incorporated
> a lot of the things from what we've gone through in
> professional development into the classroom.

Iris acknowledged that some of the professional development activities provided for teachers in her district were beneficial. "I was having such a hard time with the kids that every time I saw a brochure for a workshop about that I went," she said with a laugh.

She added that while some of the strategies indeed improved her classroom management skills, reinforcement through a longitudinal training program might have produced more comprehensive results. "Basically what you see in a workshop is like shining a flashlight in a dark room. You'll see something clearly, but not the whole picture, and then maybe it's hard to hang on to that insight or skill," she explained.

Both Gwen and James credited their principals for creating a supportive atmosphere for new teachers and for providing help in targeted areas, while other teachers pointed out the importance of formal or informal collaboration with colleagues. Charles observed that "Everybody has some knowledge, or some little technique they've used and I've been able to pick some of these things up and use them in my classroom." James agreed with Charles' assessment and added that "That's why it's good to get together with teachers and talk, because the best training of teachers is from other teachers." Iris noted that two teachers in particular provided support and suggestions that helped both with classroom management and content instruction. "The school didn't provide me with a curriculum or anything, so I didn't know what I was expected to teach." She added that a fellow language arts teacher gave her guidelines as to what material should be covered, while another teacher sat in on one of her classes and gave helpful suggestions regarding classroom management.

The topics of mentoring and professional development were not addressed by some teachers, especially those who were new to the profession. Participants appeared eager to discuss what they have learned from their students that has helped them become more effective in the classroom. At this juncture teachers provided rich data that revealed the importance accorded this topic; not only were the data more abundant, but they also exhibited striking similarities in content. Some responses spilled over into the other areas examined throughout this study, although careful analysis of linguistic content has enabled the researcher to address these student-centered topics in a sequential manner.

All participants agreed that interaction with their students provided the greatest source of knowledge about how to best build rapport and promote learning. "I've learned that you have to get to know your students first, and based on what you've learned from them and what makes their life, you pretty much have to center your classroom activities around that," Florence observed. Gwen noted the importance of ignoring negative assessments of the children in favor of forming one's own viewpoints. "Before I came to this school I was told that they're bad children and that it's a high poverty area and you're not going to be able to teach them anything," she said. "So I came here and realized that they're children with a lot of adult issues." Adam, James and Charles noted that difficulties outside of school impact a student's readiness to learn. Adam stated that when unacceptable behavior occurred,

> I felt that some of the students either had no interest in learning or didn't want to learn. You might think something's wrong with this kid, that it's just a bad kid, but what I've been learning is that sometimes there's issues at home where the students don't have a voice at all, and these kids are dealing with adult issues when they go home. Why is this kid getting sent to the office every day? You know, it's because this kid's dad is in and out of jail and nobody talks to him about it, or talks to him at home.

Adam and Charles added that it is essential for teachers to really listen to their students' concerns. "When these kids feel like they actually have a voice and feel like they're important, then their performance academically is so much better," Adam said. Charles linked listening to students with evidencing respect for them as individuals. James asserted that the first mistake many new teachers make is to "think everybody's going to be ready to learn and that there's going to be an apple sitting on your desk. When you get there you figure out that there are some kids who are just totally disconnected from anything." He explained that reasons for such oppositional attitudes may be rooted in the existence of challenges faced at home. "There's a bigger picture than what's going on right within the four walls of your classroom," he noted.

Another common source of student disengagement is the lack of reading fluency or even the lack of cultural capital necessary to make reading comprehensible. Elaine revealed that many of the male high school students who attend her program enter at a second grade reading level. "Another thing is that they have limited life experiences because of poverty," she said. "They've never even been fishing, never been on a bus, so when we try to make the material relevant, it's hard." Despite challenges like these that they must address in the classroom, many of the teachers firmly asserted their belief that all children can learn. Four teachers and the former teacher addressed the topic of relevance in instruction, as well as the importance of building on students' prior knowledge. In conjunction with building on prior knowledge, the question of what the students already know comes into play. "They possess knowledge deeper than books and the lessons," Derek noted.

Kenneth stated that

In my research I found that a teacher who was teaching math combined it with a history class and all the kids in his class got As and Bs because they saw that math was connected with their lives historically. He was teaching math off the dimensions of a pyramid in Egypt. Once the kids could see that their people created mathematics, then they were able to own it.

Since many at-risk students are particularly challenging for teachers, several participants described the ways they have adjusted their instruction to meet these students' interests and needs. Many teachers have taken the direct approach by asking students' interests and priorities at the beginning of the school year, and then incorporating elements of these into classroom instruction. When asked to identify major areas of student interest a few teachers mentioned sports or gardening, but nearly all included music as one of their students' major interests; the type of music most preferred: rap or hip hop. Surprisingly, every teacher interviewed reported utilizing at least some elements of hip hop in instruction.

Since four of the study participants are rap artists their insights regarding this phenomenon were especially insightful. Their descriptions of the use of elements of hip hop culture in instruction formed the foundation for the exploration of innovative pedagogies used by other teachers in the classroom. Each of the artists is situated in a different part of the U.S.: Adam and Derek work in cities in the South and Charles teaches in the Southwest; Kenneth was teaching in the South, although he now maintains residences in at least three cities. Each has several videos available for viewing on You Tube, a fact, they agree, that has gained them respect from their students.

Adam uses hip hop directly in his creative writing course, and reported that students became engaged with their assignments, worked productively in groups, and monitored their own and peers' behavior to ensure they would be allowed to continue writing lyrics. In conjunction with this activity Adam divided his 5th-grade students into groups and had them work collaboratively to complete assignments on rhyming, alliteration and assonance, vocabulary building, and the construction of stanzas.

Another way Adam has used hip hop with his students is by incorporating it into research projects. He chose topics such as Mississippi history, drug awareness, and recycling, and required each group to develop 10 facts about their topic through online research. "What we've been doing is actually taking those topics and the facts they gathered and we're going to write songs about them," he explained. He then produced five original beats and allowed the student group with the highest score for academic engagement and behavior management first choice, and so on down the line. Plans called for recording the groups' songs on a CD and possibly filming a music video.

Derek also uses hip hop in instruction. Two of his current music videos are particularly popular with his students, he said. One addresses the need to stay focused and work toward one's goal despite obstacles, and the other praises both the beauty and character of women. He also has a partnership with Dr. Rani Whitfield, who is known as "tha hip hop doc," to talk about health issues that affect the community and how to maintain a healthy lifestyle. For Derek's actual subject matter, however, he has not found hip hop particularly useful, citing the dearth of appropriate instructional materials as the chief reason. "I've found some materials that actually use hip hop in teaching math, but it's kind of on a more basic level," he said. "I presented it to the class to see what kind of a reaction I got and everybody gravitated toward it, but that's not things we can use in 6th, 7th and 8th grades."

In Charles' special education class, hip hop-based instruction serves as a context within which other instruction is contained. Many of his students have emotional disabilities characterized by difficulties in managing anger issues. Charles has found that through hip hop music and dance he has been able to help students learn how to utilize rhythmic movement to ameliorate the effects of their conditions. He uses hip hop across the curriculum for activities such as increasing self awareness. "I'll ask them what a favorite song means to them, when do they use the song, you know, whether it be for working out or just relaxing, does it make them angry, does it get their heart rate up," he said. "I have them write about it and describe those things to the class." He also has his students analyze contracts to determine the cost of music videos and find out "how long it really takes a rapper to start getting money, getting the big bucks." Other times he allows students to listen to hip hop radio music while they work on their assignments, a strategy he has found helps in classroom management.

> I use it as a reward. If everyone's doing their job then it stays on, but if not we cut it off and work in silence. My kids make sure that everyone is on task. They say "Make sure you're doing your work so we can listen to the radio. If you have a question, raise your hand."

For Kenneth, who has been writing and performing rap music since he was in the 6th grade, hip hop offered a way to reach his students – a notable achievement for a substitute teacher. He mentioned that each situation in which he worked differed from the others, but that he frequently was responsible for writing his own curriculum and lesson plans. He added that many of his students were familiar with his music.

> Another thing is I was one of the few teachers who could control the classroom. Once I gave them a certain level of respect, then there was no problem. They could see that I did care, but I didn't play. I had to be really, really stern at first, and then after that it was smooth sailing for the rest of the year. People have to understand that hip hop is the way that you live. The music is only one aspect of hip hop. So, yes, I could say that I used hip hop.

Teachers other than rap artists reported using hip hop as an instructional aide or as a distinct topic of study. Hip hop is integral to the programmatic structure of Elaine's after-school program.

Not only is music-making used as a creative activity, but she admits to using it as a bribe. "I have to bribe them to get to read," she said. "I use the things they love to reach them. We have to combine the academic material with their passion." She explains that the math and language arts assignments she gives her students must be completed prior to their use of the center's computers, or the audio and video equipment. She stresses the importance of having excellent teachers to work with students. "We have a hip hop artist working with the kids. His dad is in prison and his mom has gone, so he has something in common with a lot of our kids. But now he's in community college and they see him doing well."

Nationally known rap artist Bushwick Bill, a former member of the Geto Boys, also has been working closely with the center's students on their music, and Elaine says he ties his instruction into their academic work. In addition to plans for a collaborative music video with Bushwick Bill, other media-based projects included conducting interviews and filming portions of a video for the Smithsonian Institute's travel exhibition. "It gave their families a chance to see them in a whole new light," Elaine stated. "They get to show that they're good at doing something because everyone has been telling them that they're dumb and can't do anything."

Teachers such as Barbara, Helen and Iris, all of whom are older than the usual hip hop aficionado, have recognized the positive effects this musical genre seems to have on their students. Barbara, who allows her exceptional education students to listen to a hip hop radio station for 30 minutes after lunch each day, said she noticed changes in their behavior. "I saw a really great, really happy expression on their faces when they're listening to their music," she noted. She pointed out that she has used the pounding beats to help a student learn to count, and added that he demonstrated measurable retention of the knowledge acquired in this way. That same student, who was wheelchair-bound due to knee surgery, would get up and dance when he heard the music. "He'll just jump up and he's so happy," Barbara said with a smile. "He'll start clapping and doing all kinds of positive things, so I can see how the music is benefiting him, and all the rest of them." James also uses hip hop beats to help students learn complex formulas and long equations. He explained that "It's not so much that they're rapping but they learn because it has a cadence to it. You'd be amazed how much faster they learn things like that."

Helen echoed Elaine's notion of the importance of excellent teachers and role models in promoting student engagement and long-term planning strategies. She said that her student's interest in rappers manifested itself in adopting them as role models. Mississippi artist David Banner was a special favorite. "They say, 'When I grow up I want to be like David Banner.' They look at different role models, so to speak. Some of them want to be actors, doctors, just different stuff."

Florence noticed that her students were having difficulty grasping the concept of subject-verb agreement. She used an instrumental version of a hip hop song written by Ludacris and Mary J. Blige and wrote lyrics that explained the concept she wanted to teach. "I noticed that kids learn music faster, so I felt if I could incorporate music into my classroom they would be able to get the concept and learn the song at the same time," she said. Like some of the other teachers who participated in this study, Florence contrasted the motivating influence of hip hop with the stultifying effects of a lecture.

Iris agreed with this thought and gave an example of how she used hip hop to explain the concept of analogy.

I tried to explain it in all different ways, and it seemed like they were just resisting understanding of the concept. But then I played that one line from E-40's song that goes, 'We be to rap what lock is to key' and they got it immediately. It was amazing.

Adam found this result was what he would have expected.

You have to be able to reach the students where they are, you know what I mean? Give some acknowledgement to what these students are hearing every day and what they're seeing every day. If you can teach people using Shakespeare, you can teach people using Jay-Z.

All of the participants offered their recommendations for improving the content and effectiveness of formal pre-service teacher training programs. Given the line of discussion that developed during interviews regarding the efficacy of hip hop culture in instruction, participants were asked if they thought elements of hip hop should be included in these programs in some. way. Although none of the participants thought this was a poor idea, their perceptions of how it could be effectively included varied. The consensus was that hip hop awareness should be included in the university curriculum for pre-service teachers, but that its use in the classroom should be undertaken only by teachers who felt comfortable doing so. Adam and the other rap artists felt that incorporating hip hop studies into teacher training programs would be productive if done properly. Adam warned that asking teachers to work with a culture in which they are not grounded could be counterproductive. "I wouldn't suggest that a teacher who is 60 or 70 years old who hasn't studied hip hop try to use hip hop if they don't know what they're doing because it may come off corny to the kids." He suggested that "if there's a person who had my kind of role in several of the different schools, I think that would work better, as opposed to other teachers being taught how to do it." When the intent of the question was clarified, however, Adam agreed with the concept of including some elements of hip hop awareness into pre-service teacher training programs. Charles also agreed with this idea:

> I think so. Because especially if they're going to be in the
> Latino community or African American community, and
> depending on where you go, even some Asian and Caucasian
> communities. Hip hop is considered a culture and not a race
> thing. Depending on where you go, I think it's definitely
> beneficial.

Kenneth noted that "Hip hop has done more for race relations than anything." Derek voiced a similar sentiment: "I think including something about hip hop would help – definitely. Because no matter what ethnicity or class you're teaching, I think hip hop is recognized by all students of this generation, so I think it would spark their interest." Other teachers' comments were in this same vein. When asked if she agreed with the inclusion of hip hop awareness training in teacher education programs, Barbara answered, "I really do. That should be one of the strategies they learn because most students respond to music." Helen noted that "you just have to really know how to deal with the children and allow them to be the best they can be, so that would definitely be something to add." Iris' statement paralleled those of other teachers who felt including elements of hip hop culture into teacher training programs would be beneficial.

> I think that teachers need to know more about hip hop since it is like a fully formed nation where the kids all live. And if you don't speak the language of understanding with them, they will lose interest in you and in what you're trying to teach them.

Elaine offered a comment that seemed to tie in with insights gained through review of the pertinent literature.

> If they were adequately prepared, presumably they wouldn't have so much trouble in the classroom with the students' behavior. Teachers need to have respect for what kids love. A lot of them, they'll feel intimidated by hip hop and they feel it's fluff. They feel hip hop is in the middle of the fluff and it strikes at morality. So give them some tools to defend it and keep it simple. They may feel they don't have control over the subject, but they should be facilitators. Let the kids be the teacher and you'll have clear sailing.

Other important areas of recommendations for adding to the teacher training curriculum addressed issues of technology, special education, and more extensive inclusion of teacher candidates in actual classroom instructional activities. James stressed the role of technology in instruction, noting that students have grown up with technology. "They feel comfortable with it, and if you're not using it they'll wonder why." He added that adapting to technological innovations is essential, but apparently difficult for younger teachers as well as veteran teachers.

> That's probably the biggest gap we have right now. People may know how to use i-chat or Twitter, but nobody's trained you on how this can be implemented in the classroom. If you don't explain to somebody how they can use it, it just kind of sits there.

Gwen reinforced James' statement by noting that

I don't think we should get away from all the paper and pencils, but at the same time you can't limit it to that because that's not the age we're in. Some teachers don't want to change, but it's either change or we lose them.

Adam summarized this point of view succinctly:

As technology and the media are changing, why do schools do the same thing as it was 50 or 60 years ago? The world is moving so fast, but it seems to be moving a little bit slower in the school district.

Three participants suggested other topics for inclusion in teacher training. Barbara addressed the necessity of including more extensive coverage of exceptional education issues into teacher training since most of these students are included in regular education classes. "I would really stress that because I see student teachers coming out now and they see the special kids and they go, 'Oh, my God!' They don't know what to do, and here they are, 4th-year college students." She also recommended greater emphasis on learning styles to meet the needs of all students, and noted that hip hop might have a role here as well. "I've seen how music affects them. Music is very good because our kids respond to music." Florence suggested that university programs for pre-service teachers should create greater opportunities for classroom immersion. She also noted that these pre-service teachers might be able to provide classroom teachers with valuable feedback. Helen, on the other hand, stressed the need for more help with the preparation of high-quality lesson plans. "We didn't write lesson plans in college and that's one of the things that I feel the college should do."

Emerging Themes

During the analysis of participants' responses, several themes emerged from the data. The researcher was careful to look for data that contradicted the inference of these themes, but it seemed clear that they were strongly rooted in both the content and context of their occurrence. Emergent themes may be categorized under two broad headings: those that related to student characteristics and needs, and those that addressed teacher effectiveness. It is important to note, however, that the main emphasis was on promoting students' engagement and overall success, and virtually all of the conversations remained student-focused. Six major themes were identified: three relating to students, and three pertinent to discussions of teacher effectiveness. Student-centered themes included: student engagement, relevance of instructional materials and pedagogies, and the centrality of hip hop culture in students' lives. The three themes pertaining to teachers were: the importance of knowing students as individuals, strategies for promoting student engagement, and significant recommendations for teacher training programs. Each of these will be presented in sequence, although their interrelated nature must be noted as well.

Engagement

All participants in this study either stated or alluded to the necessity of engaging students as partners in their own learning. The consensus was that if teachers fail to engage students, then they lose them. From participants' statements on this point, it may be inferred that student engagement may help to decrease dropout rates and the subsequent conditions that often ensue. Elaine, for example, stated that "The idea and real goal of this is to keep them from dropping out and going to jail."

An element related to student engagement was that of critical thinking skills. Elaine mentioned that critical thinking is not taught in schools, but is essential for the development of decision-making competency. Barbara pointed out that she frequently asks students' opinions to help them sharpen this skill, and Iris commented on the necessity of "teaching them to think for themselves, not just memorize things."

Relevance

There was consensus among interviewees regarding the necessity of relevance in promoting student engagement and persistence. This was overtly stated by several teachers, while others alluded to it. Gwen, for example, developed an approach she termed Real World. One manifestation of this has been a store in the classroom where each Friday students can purchase items with scrip they have earned for activities such as providing peer tutoring, helping out in the classroom, or answering higher-order questions. When gasoline prices increased significantly, Gwen raised the prices in the classroom store and used that as a lesson with students. Another way Gwen employs the real-world concept is through reminding students of the need for persistence in overcoming obstacles. "When they get frustrated about something I tell them it's ok to be frustrated, but are you going to make decisions and move on, or are you going to allow it to shut you down?" Her rationale for this focus is the element of relevance.

I'm just trying to make the classroom as real as possible. I try to help them find value in coming to school. It's not just coming to school to take tests. I tell them at some point the tests and scores are not going to matter; what's going to matter is what you've learned, lessons that you can take beyond the classroom.

Centrality of Hip Hop Culture

Despite the differences in race and gender and the age gaps among participants, all acknowledged the centrality of hip hop music and culture to their students' lives. In general, teachers described the ease with which students learn and retain material, as well as the apparent joy they experience when this interest is acknowledged and nurtured. They also noted how quickly students master new concepts through this medium. No participant reported having students who were unfamiliar with or disengaged from this genre, and several acknowledged that it was a key to overcoming student alienation and apathy. Teachers noted that the judicious use of hip hop-based instruction resulted in student engagement, attainment and retention of knowledge. Several felt that using hip hop directly with students allowed them to simultaneously address students' interests and to access their prior knowledge.

Importance of Knowing Students as Individuals

Virtually all interviewees stated the importance of getting to know one's students as individuals. They described this process in terms of eliciting information about students' likes and dislikes, their priorities, and salient details about their lives. Gwen described a situation where a boy's behavior was unacceptable and he resisted compliance with teacher directives. She noted that when she allowed him to write what he chose he explained that he had been having a very difficult time outside of school. "It was only Tuesday, but he said he'd had a bad week," she added.

Others noted how their young students were struggling with adult issues such as a parent's incarceration, drug addiction, or willful absence from the child's life. In conjunction with this theme, teachers also mentioned the importance of creating a nurturing, safe environment where children can flourish. Elaine's point about the lack of cultural capital also is relevant here and ties in with Gwen's observation that "You have to figure out where they are so you can meet them and then take them where they need to be."

Strategies for Promoting Student Engagement

Several participants noted the success they had achieved through participatory activities which allowed students to move, talk and explore, and to introduce topics of interest to themselves. This was discussed in the context of building students' critical thinking and problem-solving abilities often in a setting requiring teamwork. A side benefit to this, some noted, was the reduction of classroom management issues. "I'm not here to be a disciplinarian," Adam stated.

Recommendations for Teacher Training Programs

In general, participants' recommendations for teacher training programs were student focused and centered around the themes outlined above. Five points emerged as most frequent or significant: the inclusion of some form of hip hop awareness training, expanded and longitudinal training in the creative use of instructional technology, additional training in addressing the needs of exceptional students, immersion of pre-service teachers in real classroom settings, and work in the development of effective lesson plans. "At least some exposure to these kinds of things could have saved me a lot of grief," Iris noted.

Another recommendation for teacher training was alluded to,

but not stated specifically. Since so many teachers stressed the need for acquiring deep knowledge of students as individuals, it might be reasonable to infer that they would favor the inclusion of coursework that addressed the characteristics and behaviors of at-risk students – especially those who come from a background of generational poverty. Florence stated that her university training did not address this issue at all, and Charles added that, although his coursework had included issues of cultural and socioeconomic difference, the political realities of test-driven instruction precluded the implementation of strategies to accommodate these differences. He emphasized that "Because of No Child Left Behind I don't think we're addressing their actual needs."

On the state of hip-hop today, what's changed for the better and what's changed for the worse?

I don't think it's changed much at all. There's still kids from the ghetto, writing stories and poetry about that struggle. It's a little more sophisticated now, because their poetry is not only about where they came from, but it's about their journey. But there's also new art that is coming out of this real place where people are voiceless. The big voices are the ones that have seen that struggle and express it in an interesting way. It's a good look inside the minds of people who would otherwise be silent. They would still be there, but they would not have a voice. So these voices are the same, they come from struggle and describe a part of America that was not celebrated or understood before. It's a part of the American consciousness. And now, here they are influencing and speaking directly to the most powerful people in the world.

Russell Simmons
Interview
Color Magazine
2011

6 CONSIDERING A HIP HOP CURRICULUM

In discussing the major findings of this study, each research question is stated followed by a review of how participants' responses answered the questions. Participants' responses also are viewed in terms of whether each confirms or contrasts with the literature. By comparing the findings of this study to previous studies, it is clear that the data derived from interviews with participants confirm many of the theories and perspectives found in the literature. It should be noted, however, that many insights provided by interviewees extended beyond those gleaned from published works and, therefore, serve as contributions to the body of knowledge on this essential topic.

Research Question 1

How does formal teacher training prepare teachers to meet students' needs?

Even among participants who rated their pre-service training favorably, there was agreement that many needed elements were not provided. According to Levine (2006), the criteria by which teacher training programs should be evaluated include: programmatic offerings aligned with the needs of schools, teachers and students; curricular coherence targeted to the needs of teachers at specific types of schools; and a balanced approach to instruction that combines theory and practice.

The data collected during this study indicated that these criteria were not being fully met. Several teachers said they would have benefited from additional training in addressing students' different learning styles and other needs. Many insightful comments from teachers paralleled the theories presented by Payne (2005) and Jacob (2007) who discussed at length ways to bridge the gap that often exists between teachers and their at-risk students. Teachers repeatedly stressed the importance of getting to know students individually and building relationships of mutual understanding and respect, and reported with distain instances in which teachers frequently yelled at students in attempts to control their behavior. Seltzer (2007) also pointed out the vast gap that often develops between middle-class teachers and their at-risk students. Charles' comments supported this assertion:

> There are cultural limitations that are preventing students from grasping the knowledge and the information they need to be successful. A lot of our recruiting is in the Midwest, so we have teachers from Wisconsin, upper Michigan, Iowa, and then the students that they are teaching are on the low end of the socioeconomic status. You know, parents are in jail, drugs, there's all kinds of things that are going on.

Elaine and some other participants described the dismay they felt when confronted with the paucity of at-risk students' basic knowledge and skills, and their disengagement from the educational process. This same phenomenon has been studied by researchers such as Payne (2005), Thompson and Smith (2005), and Bonny, Britto, Klostermann, Hornung and Slap (2000). Data provided by participants who remarked that their pre-service training "helped a little bit" or "didn't help at all" were similar to findings reported in the literature as well (Seltzer, 2007).

Some of the literature addressing the topic of effective teacher training models evaluated the benefits of the 5-year professional development school, but results were inconclusive (Huntley, 2008). Since none of the teachers interviewed in this study had attended a program of this type, there were no data that addressed this issue. It may be cautiously inferred, however, that since participants spoke of the need to have more opportunities to teach in actual classroom settings prior to graduation, that they would have been in agreement with Robinson and Spooner (2004) and others who discussed the strong component of sustained classroom experience that characterizes this model.

Research Question 2

The second research question asked, How does experiential training affect teacher preparedness? A few participants chose to discuss professional development activities such as seminars and workshops, which they reported were useful and gave them additional strategies for working with students. Others felt that formal or informal mentoring could be helpful, but only if the mentor's ideas were current. These points align with findings reported by Ahuja (2007), Haberman (2008), and Jacob (2007). Administrators were deemed a significant source of support and guidance, but other teachers were viewed as especially helpful sources of knowledge due to their actual classroom experience. A common perspective that emerged from the data, however, was that teachers had to figure out on their own how to best achieve effectiveness in the classroom, and how to best manage behavioral issues (Seltzer, 2007). All teachers interviewed felt that their main source of experiential knowledge was students themselves; discussion of this point are addressed below.

Research Question 3

The question, How do the characteristics of students from diverse backgrounds impact teacher preparedness? was especially fruitful. Participants utilized this opportunity to examine and explain their relationships with students, and the elements necessary for successfully engaging them in the educational process. Many study participants raised the point that teachers need to acquire a deep understanding of students' backgrounds in order to build relationships of mutual trust and respect that may offset students' alienation from the educational process. Whitcomb and Borko (2006), Payne (2008), and Hill (2009) are a few of the many researchers who have emphasized the need for teachers to have knowledge of the factors shaping their students' lives, as well as their interests. Such knowledge of students is essential, participants noted, especially in light of the fact that students may have elements of their lives that distract and distance them from academic pursuits. Similar lines of discussion were presented in the work of Bonny, Britto, Klosterman, Hornung, and Slap (2000); Comissiong (2007); and Wlodkowski and Ginsberg (1995).

Participants and researchers noted the efficacy of accessing students' prior knowledge and incorporating it into instruction. In this context the notion of relevance was introduced. Several teachers mentioned the importance of getting to know students as individuals, and that this involved knowing their interests and priorities. One participant observed that teachers need to first determine what knowledge students do not have in order to help them build cultural and social capital. These insights are especially well supported in the literature by researchers such as Dyson (2007), Freire (2007), Hill (2009), Payne (2005), Payne (2008), and Stovall (2008).

Research Question 4

What recommendations do teachers propose to inform practice and enhance preparedness? This research question also generated numerous insights and potentially useful suggestions regarding the content of teacher training programs. As discussed in Chapter 4, some of the main recommendations found in the data were: provide an extended component of teaching in actual classrooms during the pre-service program, include more instruction on student learning styles, and identification of other student characteristics, including attention to their likes and dislikes. One participant argued well for more thorough training for work with exceptional education students.

Although the researcher has admitted that a limitation of this study was a bias toward the efficacy of including elements of hip hop culture as pedagogy, the degree of participants' agreement with this approach was unexpected. Nine of the 11 participants recommended that hip hop awareness should be included in the curriculum of formal teacher training programs offered at the college or university level. The tenth participant did not disagree with these suggestions, but did not mention it himself, although he was using hip hop in his own math classes. Kenneth, the former teacher who is a rap artist, focused more on the need for relevance in instruction, and stressed that teachers should be themselves and know how to connect material across the curriculum. However, he did allow that hip hop awareness training for teachers might have merit.

> I don't think that teachers have to be rapping in the classroom. I don't believe that. It's about that connection to whatever subject you're talking about. But I think that every aspect that will help teachers relate is important. We need to try something though, you know?

The methodology of this study, which relied on a snowballing technique to identify potential participants, may account for some of these results since it would be expected that teachers might recommend others who shared their views. Despite these limitations, the findings still may be considered important since all participants, regardless of age, gender or ethnicity, were currently using – or had used – hip hop in some way to boost student engagement, add relevance, and augment retention of knowledge. These findings might not surprise other researchers, however. Hip hop scholars such as Hill (2009), Morgan (2002), and Dyson (2007) have noted the efficacy of utilizing the positive motivators of hip hop in instruction; similar points were made by Coomes and DeBard (2004) and Garcia (2002). A wealth of journal articles have reported on studies that measured the outcome of this pedagogy with K-12 students, especially at-risk urban youth (Ahuja, 2007; Caruthers, 2006; Darby & Shelby, 2005; Duncan-Andrade & Morrell, 2005; Green, 2008; Jasper, 2008; Smitherman, 2002). Several articles were located that were based in a negative view of hip hop, but these did not address the topic of using it in instruction; from the content and tone of these articles, the reader would be safe in assuming that these researchers might question such an approach (Adams & Fuller, 2009; Oware, 2007; Sullivan, 2003). Kenneth addressed the potential objections to the use of hip hop in education at any level. "Some people don't like us anyway, so they don't believe what we do has any merit," he noted.

Implications for Policy and Practice

During the course of the interviews the data corroborated the findings of Coomes and DeBard (2004) who discussed characteristics of the millennial generation. Since the literature supported study participants' comments and opinions it becomes necessary to examine current educational policies, especially those that center around punitive measures rather than the development of the interpersonal partnerships needed to facilitate change. Various sources agree that education should include the development of students' critical thinking skills. Through changes in legislative mandates, the focus on test preparation could be expanded beyond current parameters. A shift in focus toward more holistic notions of achievement and accountability would be a productive outcome. An added benefit of this policy change would be the preclusion of further state incursions into areas where government policy contradicts practitioner knowledge.

A particularly interesting finding of this study was that some teachers who lacked or had not completed teacher training programs seemed to fare very well in the classroom; all of these teachers were using elements of hip hop in instruction. It would behoove policy makers to note this point and to set forth a framework within which collaborative discussions could occur. The definition of the term Highly Qualified Teacher might need to be expanded as well.

The implementation of these augmented policies could be productive of invigorating perspectives on the content and context of the curriculum at all levels. Two of the hip hop educators who participated in this study described their effect on other teachers who noted the success they had in engaging students, disarming behavioral issues, and fostering real learning. Some other participants mentioned that a few other teachers at their school were utilizing this pedagogy as well. Backed by the data and literature discussed throughout, new modules could be developed to include hip hop awareness training in the curriculum for pre-service teachers. This is perhaps the most important recommendation since the research referenced above indicates the importance of this culture to students, and the ways in which it informs individuals' identity and life-style choices. As discussed thoroughly above, the findings of this study support this assertion.

Other programmatic designs could include the establishment of hip hop studies as an option at appropriate points during the high-school experience; cross-curricular options abound. The design and establishment of a program of this type at the university level opens another area for application of policies revised in accordance with the tenets outlined above.

Recommendations for Future Research

Due to the characteristics of millennial students discussed throughout and the fast-paced changes occurring in national and global society, it is important to design educational offerings that meet students' interests and needs, while still maintaining rigor and high expectations for achievement. Additional research is warranted in several areas, both to compare with the findings of this study and to explore beyond its confines. Qualitative studies to examine the perspectives of pre-service teachers and to explore the experiences and views of students toward their education could characterize the next level of research in this field. Strategic planning activities could benefit from an amplified examination of the nature of the university partnerships with K-12 districts, and perhaps students could provide input to the university for program design.

Since the teacher attrition rate was identified in Chapter 1 as a major concern, studies that examine factors that lead to, or help alleviate, this trend would be useful. Other foci of qualitative studies could include curriculum design for different student grade and content levels, other innovative pedagogies that could be combined with the use of hip hop in instruction, and inventive forms of teacher-student-community collaboration. This study also may serve as a springboard for quantitative studies involving the comparison of dropout rates prior to and after the implementation of specific interactive pedagogies, changes in graduation rates in schools where innovations are utilized, and surveys of teacher and student opinions about the educational process.

It also would be germane to these types of inquiries to further examine the content and process of current teacher training programs, to include investigations into the process of curricular change at the university level, and to analyze how these processes promote or hinder the appropriateness of instructional content in teacher training programs. It is likely that successful models for teacher instruction exist, and study of these would add to the discussion of this important topic.

The appropriate use of media – both in terms of student

consumption and use – offer myriad opportunities for the development of meaningful studies. Since the efficacy of employing elements of hip hop in instruction emerged as an important theme, the relationship between hip hop based instruction and knowledge retention, and the relationship between hip hop based instruction and student achievement on standardized tests provide areas ripe for additional examination. A study questioning teachers' views toward inclusion of this pedagogy would be illustrative, as would studies examining school administrators' views on how best to promote student retention, achievement and graduation rates. Finally, the inclusion of non-teachers as partners in instruction within the regular classroom could be examined and discussed in terms of school-community partnerships, and the role this may play in the acquisition of students' – and teachers' – cultural capital.

A research design featuring triangulation of data could be used to compare and then extend the findings of this study. The three cultures that could be addressed could include those of the students, the K-12 system, and that of the higher education community. Three taxonomical objectives could include student engagement and achievement, teacher learning as reflected in an increase of perceived and measurable preparedness and effectiveness, and teacher-training program development and coordination at the higher education level. This model could be particularly fruitful in providing data to drive curriculum development at the K-12 level as well as in higher education.

The researcher, of course, would most like to see a replication or extension of this study. Possible applications could involve examination of the views of hip hop industry professionals toward collaboration with curriculum-writing projects at the K-12 and university levels, examination of the research questions addressed here in other locations and settings, and attitudes toward hip hop instruction in other countries. If this were to occur, the researcher would most likely plan to work with other investigators to help develop insights that would benefit the students most in need of support and encouragement.

Conclusion

The initial purpose of this study was to illuminate teachers' perceptions of preparedness after completing a teacher training program at a college or university and working in a classroom with students of their own. Analysis of the findings has indicated that, based on participant-generated data, many current teacher training programs are inadequate in preparing new teachers for the realities they face in working with at-risk urban youth. It should be noted again that several teachers who had no formal pre-service training were achieving high levels of success with their students in terms of student engagement, behavior and academic success. This serves as a strong indictment of teacher training programs that should not be ignored.

Due to the preference among millennial generation students for collaboration and team work, their familiarity with and preference for the use of technology, and the degree to which text and images contained in hip hop culture influence their lives, it may be concluded that the inclusion of these elements into formal teacher training programs is warranted. The recurrent theme of knowing one's students through gaining an understanding and appreciation for their likes, dislikes and interests informs this discussion as well. Since the use of hip hop in various ways in instruction was another theme that emerged during analysis of the data, it may be concluded that there would be merit in including hip hop awareness training into formal teacher training programs.

It also could be inferred that the implementation of hip hop-based education projects in the nonprofit sector could have positive effects on student retention, graduation, and post-secondary plans. Conferences, workshops, artist showcases and other events could bring professors, rap artists, students, and young people who have dropped out of school together in a joyous celebration of education that bridges chasms between generations and socioeconomic classes. Utilizing the power inherent in hip hop culture to reach and teach those most in need of educational and social support could prove a way to help community stakeholders ensure that no child is ever left behind.

CAROL A. O'CONNOR, PHD

You can't write a book if you've never read a book. And if you've read five books and you try to write a book, your book will mainly encompass the themes and the context of the five books you've read. Now, the more books you read, the more you can bring to a book when you decide to write one. So the more rap I learned, the more I was able to bring to rap when I decided to rap. But this was all subconscious.

Bun B

CAROL A. O'CONNOR, PHD

7 REFERENCES

Adams, T.M. & Fuller, D.B. (2007). The words have changed but the ideology remains the same: Misogynistic lyrics in rap music. *Journal of Black Studies 36*, 936-957. Retrieved November 20, 2007 from http:// jbs.sagepub.com.

Ahuja, R. (2007, March). Towards an understanding of excellence in urban pedagogy. A portrait of a high school. *The Qualitative Report, 12*(10), 1-19.

Allen, M. (2003). Eight questions on teacher preparation: What does the research say? Denver, CO: Education Commission of the States.

Alliance for Excellent Education (2005, August). Teacher attrition: A costly loss to the nation and to the states. Retrieved November 25, 2007 from http:/www.all4ed.org.

Altheide, D., and Johnson, J. (1994). Criteria for assessing interpretive validity in qualitative research. In N. Denzin and Y. Lincoln (Eds.) *Handbook of Qualitative Research*, Thousand Oaks, CA: Sage.

Arizona Department of Education (2009). Retrieved June 28, 2009 from http://www.ade.state.az.us.

Berry, B., & Norton, J. (2006, July). Wild kids, demanding administrators, the NCLB. *Edutopia.* retrieved from http://www.edutopia.org/learn-masters.

Biernacki, B. & Waldorf, D. (1981, November). Snowball sampling problems and techniques of chain referral sampling. *Sociological Methods & Research, 10*(2). 141-143.

Boe, E.E., Cook, L.H., & Sunderland, R.J. (2006). Attrition of beginning teachers: Does teacher preparation matter?. Center for Research and Evaluation in Social Policy. University of Pennsylvania, Research Report No. 2006-TSDQ2.

Boe, E.E., Shin, S., & Cook, L.H. (2007). What makes a great teacher? *Journal of Special Education, 41*(3), 158-170.

Bonny, M., Britto, M.T., Klostermann, B.K., Hornung, R.W., & Slap, G.B. (2000). School disconnectedness: Identifying adolescents at risk. *Pediatrics,* 106, 1017-1021.

Bryson, J.M. (2004). *Strategic Planning for Public and Nonprofit Organizations.* San Francisco: Jossey-Bass.

Burke-Adams, A. (2004). The benefits of equalizing standards and creativity: Discovering a balance in instruction. *Gifted Child Today, 30*(1). 58-63.

Bush, G.W., (2001). No Child Left Behind Act of 2001. Retrieved December 10, 2007 from http://www.whitehouse.gov/news/reports/no-child-left-behind.html.

Cabrera, A.F., & LaNasa, S.M. (2000). Understanding the college-choice process. *New Directions for Institutional Research, 107,* 5-22.

Caruthers, L. (2006, Fall). Using storytelling to break the silence that binds us to sameness in our schools. *The Journal of Negro Education.* Retrieved August 15, 2008 from http://findarticles.com/p/articles/mi_200610/ai_18705759.

Chang, J. (2005). *Can't Stop Won't Stop.* New York: Picador.

Cherubini, L., (2006). Speaking up and speaking freely: Beginning teachers' critical perceptions of their professional induction. *The Professional Educator*. Retrieved March 8, 2008 from http://education.auburn.edu/centersandinstitutes/ trumanpierceinstitute/theprofessionaleducator/html.

Cherubini, L. (2008, Spring). Teacher-candidates' perceptions of schools as professional communities of inquiry: A mixed-methods investigation. The Professional Educator, 32(1), retrieved August 21, 2008 from http://education.auburn.edu/centersandinstitutes/trumanpi erceinstitute/theprofessionaleducator/html.

Cicariello-Maher, G. (2007). A critique of Du Boisian reason: Kanye West and the fruitfulness of double-consciousness. *Journal of Black Studies*. Retrieved November 17, 2007 from http://jbs.sagepub.com.

Cohen, A.M. (1998). *The Shaping of American Higher Education*. San Francisco: Jossey-Bass Publishers.

Comissiong, S,W.F. (2007). *Mining the Positive Motivators from Hip Hop to Educate*. Bloomington, IN: Xlibris Press.

Coomes, M.D. & DeBard, R. (Eds.) (2004). *Serving the Millennial Generation*. San Francisco: Jossey Bass.

Creswell, J.W. (1998). *Qualitative Inquiry and Research Design: Choosing Among Five Traditions*. Thousand Oaks, CA: Sage.

Creswell, J.W. (2003). *Research Design: Qualitative, Quantitative, and Mixed Method Approaches*. Thousand Oaks, CA: Sage.

Creswell, J.W. (2008). *Educational Research*. Upper Saddle River, NJ: Pearson.

Cushman, K. (2007). *Fires in the Bathroom: Advice for Teachers from High School Students*. New York: The New Press.

Darby, D., & Shelby, T. (Eds,). (2005). *Hip Hop and Philosophy: Rhyme 2 Reason.* Chicago: Open Court.

Darling-Hammond, L., & McLaughlin, M.W. (2003). Policies that support professional development in an era of reform. National College for School Leadership. Retrieved June 15, 2008 from http://www.ncsl.org.uk/publications.

Denzin, N.K. & Lincoln, Y.S. (Eds.). (2000). *Handbook of Qualitative Research.* London:Sage Publications.

Denzin, N.K. & Lincoln, Y.S. (Eds.). (2003).*Collecting and Interpreting Qualitative Materials.* Thousand Oaks, CA: Sage Publications.

Denzin, N.K. & Lincoln, Y.S. (Eds.). (2005). *The SAGE Handbook of Qualitative Research* (3rd Ed.). Thousand Oaks, CA: Sage.

Duncan-Andrade, J.M.R., & Morrell, E. (2005, May). Turn up that radio, teacher: Popular cultural pedagogy in new century urban schools. *Journal of School Leadership. 15,* 284-308.

Dyson, M.E. (2007). *Know What I Mean?.* New York: Basis Civitas Books.

Fass, S. & Cauthen, N.K. (2007, November) Who are America's poor children? The official story. National Center for Children in Poverty. Retrieved November 25, 2007, from http://www.nccp.org.

Fisher, E.J. (2005, Summer). Black student achievement and the oppositional culture model. *The Journal of Negro Education,* retrieved October 25, 2007 from http://findarticles.com/p/articles/mi_qa3626/is_200507/ai_15743650.

Foote, C.J. (2005). The challenge and potential of high-need urban education. *The Journal of Negro Education, 74*(4). 237-245.

Freire, P. (2007). *Pedagogy of the Oppressed.* New York: Continuum.

Garcia, E. (2002) *Student Cultural Diversity*. Boston: Houghton Mifflin Co.

Gardner, H. (1993). *Frames of Mind: The Theory of Multiple Intelligences*. New York: Basic Books.

Gardner, H. (2006). *Five Minds for the Future*. Boston: Harvard Business School Press.

George, N. (1998). *Hip Hop America*. New York: Penguin Books.

Giallo, R., & Little, E. (2003). Classroom behaviour problems: The relationship between preparedness, classroom experiences, and self-efficacy in graduate and student teachers. *Australian Journal of Educational and Developmental Psychology, 3*, 21-34.

Ginswright, S.A. (2004). *Black in School*. New York: Teachers College Press.

Guba, E.G. & Lincoln, Y.S. (1981). *Effective Evaluation: Improving the Usefulness of Evaluation Results through Responsive and Naturalistic Approaches*. San Francisco, CA:Jossey-Bass.

Gonzalez, L., Brown, M.S., & Slate, J.R. (2008, March). Teachers who left the teaching profession: A qualitative understanding. *The Qualitative Report, 13*(1), 1-11.

Green, K. (2008). Check it: Reflections on hip hop and education. In T. F. Roy (Ed.). *The Hip Hop Education Guidebook*. New York: Hip Hop Association.

Haberman, M. (2008, Summer). Gentle teaching in a violent society. *Educational Horizons*. Retrieved May 21, 2008 from http://www.pilambda.org/horizons/volumes.html.

Hall, H.R. (2007, Winter). Poetic expressions: Students of color express resiliency through metaphors and similes. *Journal of Advanced Academics, 18*(2)., 216-244.

Hamilton, K. (2004, April). Making some noise: The academy's hip hop generation – scholarship on the genre moves beyond a project of legitimization into a more self-critical, challenging realm. *Black Issues in Higher Education 21*(5), 34.

Harrison, Jr., L., Moore, L.N., & Evans, L. (2006). Ear to the streets: The race, hip-hop, and sports learning communities at Louisiana State University. *Journal of Black Studies, 36*, 662-634.

Henderson, E.A. (1996). Slouching toward Bork: The culture wars and self-criticism in hip-hop music. *Journal of Black Studies*, 26, 308-339.

Henderson, H. (2004). School of rap: The politics and pedagogies of rap music. UMI No. 3147625.

Henderson-Sparks, J., Paredes, L.N., & Gonzales, D. (2002, Winter). Student teacher   preparation: A collaborative model to assist at-risk students. *Preventing School Failure, 46*(2). 80-85.

Hill, M.L. (2009). *Beats, Rhymes, and Classroom Life*. New York: Teachers College Press.

Hoepfl, M.C. (1997, Fall). Choosing qualitative research: A primer for technology education researchers. *Journal of Technology Education*. Retrieved November 16, 2007 from http:scholar.lib.vt.edu/ejournals/JTE/v9nl/hoepfl.html.

Hossler, D., Schmidt, J., & Vesper, N. (1999). *How Social, Economic and Educational Factors Influence the Decisions Students Make*. Baltimore, MD: The John Hopkins University Press.

Huntley, H. (2008, April). Teachers' work: Beginning teachers conceptions of competence. *The Australian Educational Researcher, 35*(1). 125-145.

Iwamoto, D. (2003, Summer). Tupac Shakur: Understanding the identity formation of hyper-masculinity of a popular hip hop artist. *The Black Scholar, 33*(2), 44-49.

Jacob, B.A. (2007, Spring). The challenges of staffing urban schools with effective teachers. *The Future of Children, 17*(1), 129-153.

Jasper, K. (2009). The lesson 2.0. In T.F. Roy (Ed.). *The Hip Hop Education Guidebook*. New York: Hip Hop Association.

Johnson, B.J. (2006). "Getting started": The role of institutional orientations and collegial support in new faculty socialization. *Journal of the Professoriate, 1*, 23-43.

Kagan, D.M. (1990). How schools alienate students at risk: A model for examining proximal classroom variables. *Educational Psychologist, 25*. Retrieved November 20, 2007 from http://www.questia.com/googleScholar.qst. jsessionid=HD1bFS2T.

Kitwana, B. (2002). *The Hip Hop Generation*. New York: Basic Civitas Books.

Kitwana, B. (2005), *Why White Kids Love Hip Hop*. New York: Basic Civitas Group.

Koch, W. (2007, November 16). Study charts number of children who go hungry or are at risk, *USA Today*, 18A.

Kozol, J. (2005). *The Shame of the Nation: The Restoration of Apartheid Schooling in America*. New York: Crown Publishers.

Levine, A. (2006). Educating school teachers. *The Education Schools Project*. Retrieved November 27, 2007 from ww.edschools.org.

Lincoln, Y.S. & Guba, E.G. (1985). *Naturalistic Inquiry*. Newbury Park, CT: Sage Publications.

Liston, D., Whitcomb, J., & Borko, H. (2006). Too little or too much: Teacher preparation and the first years of teaching. *Journal of Teacher Education, 57*(4), 351-358.

Louisiana Department of Education (2009). Retrieved June 28, 2009 from http://www.doe.state,la.us.

Marbley, A.F., Bonner, F.A., McKisick, S., Henfield, M.S., & Watts, L.M. (2007, Spring). Interfacing cultural specific pedagogy with counseling: A proposed diversity training model for preparing preservice teachers for diverse learners. *Multicultural Education.* Retrieved November 20, 2007 from http://findarticles.com/p/articles/mi_qa3935/is_200704/ai_n19198579.

Marshall, C. & Rossman, G.B. (2006). *Designing Qualitative Research.* Thousand Oaks, CA: Sage Publications.

Marshall, G. (1998). Snowballing technique. *A Dictionary of Sociology.* Retrieved April 17, 2009 from http://www.encyclopedia.com.

McDonough, P. (1997), *Choosing colleges: How social class and schools structure opportunity.* New York: SUNY Press.

McKinney, S.E., Robinson, J., & Spooner, M. (2004). A comparison of urban teacher characteristic for student interns placed in different urban school settings. *The Professional Educator,* 26(2), 17-30.

Mississippi: Demographics and the economy (2008). Retrieved May 20, 2009 from http://www.statehealthfacts.org.

Mississippi Department of Education (2009). Retrieved June 28, 2009 from http://www.mde.k12.ms.us.

Mississippi poverty rate data (2009). Retrieved May 20, 2009 from http://www.city-data.com/poverty/povertyMississippi.html.

Morgan, M. (2002). *Language, Discourse and Power in African American Culture.* New York: Cambridge University Press.

National Center for Education Statistics (2001). Teacher quality: A report on the preparation and qualifications of public school teachers (NCES Publication No. 1999080). Retrieved September 18, 2007 from http:llnces.ed.gov/surveys.

NCCP (2008). 10 important questions about child poverty and family economic hardship. Retrieved July 7, 2998 from http://www.nccp.org/pages/pdf.

NCATE (2001). Standards for professional development schools. NCATE document.

Ogbar, J.O.G. (1999). Slouching toward Bork: The culture wars and self-criticism in hip hop music. *Journal of Black Studies*, 30, 164-183.

Oware, M. (2007). A 'man's woman'? Contradictory messages in the songs of female rappers, 1992-2000. *The Journal of Black Studies*. Retrieved November 20, 2007 from http:// jbs.sagepub.com.

Patton, M. & Kritsonis (2006, November). The law of increasing returns: A process for retaining teachers – national recommendations. *Doctoral Forum*, *3*(1), 1-9.

Payne, R. K., (2005). *A framework for Understanding Poverty*. Highlands, TX: aha! Process, Inc.

Payne, R.K. (2008, April). Nine powerful practices: Nine strategies help raise the achievement of students living in poverty. *Educational Leadership*, *65* (7), 48-52.

Perry, I. (2004). *Prophets of the Hood*. Durham, NC: Duke University Press.

Pimderhughes, H. (1997). *Race in the Hood*. Minneapolis: University of Minnesota Press.

Price, E.G. (2007, August). What's new? The effect of hip hop culture on everyday English. Retrieved April 11, 2008 from http://www.america.gov/st/diversity.

Powell, K. (2008). *Someday We'll All Be Free.* New York: Soft Skull Press.

Qualitative Research Methods: A Data Collector's Field Guide (n.d.). Family Health International. Retrieved April 14, 2009 from http://www.fhi.org.pdf+research +technique+snowballing.

Reed, J. & Black, D.J. (2006, Winter). Toward a pedagogy of transformative teacher education. *Multicultural Education,* 34-39.

Relic, P. (2007, December). Gotta say it. *XXL Magazine,* 74-80. Researcher points to pop culture for educating black youth. (2002). *Black Issues in Higher Education, 19.* 18.

Rockwell, S. (2007, Fall). Working smarter, not harder: Reaching the tough to teach. *Kappa Delta Pi Record,* 8-12.

Rose, T. (1994). *Black Noise: Rap Music and Black Culture in Contemporary America.* Middletown, CT: Wesleyan University Press.

Rose, T. (2008). *The Hip Hop Wars: What We Talk about When We Talk About Hip Hop and Why It Matters.* New York: Basic Books.

Rubenstein, G. (2007). The Edutopia poll. Retrieved November 30, 2007 from http://www.edutopia.org/node/5035.

Runnell, M. (2008). The organic connection between hip hop and social justice education: A theoretical model for activism. In F. T. Roy (Ed.). *The Hip Hop Education Guide Book.* New York: Hip Hop Association.

Samy, A.H. (2007). Critical hip hop language pedagogies: combat, consciousness, and the cultural politics of communication. *Journal of Language, Identity, and Education, 6*(2), 161-176.

Seltzer, S. (2007). Minding the gap. Retrieved September 23, 2007, from http://www.wiretap.org/education/43246.

Shenton, A.K. (2004). Strategies for ensuring trustworthiness in qualitative research projects. *Education for Information,* 63-75.

Smitherman, G. (2002). *Black Talk: From the Hood to the Amen Corner.* New York: Houghton Mifflin Co.

Smokler, D. (2005). *Making Learning Come Alive.* San Diego, CA: The Brain Store. State population data (2008). Retrieved May 20, 2009 from http://www.census.gov/population.html.

Stevenson, J.M., Crockett, W., Jefferson, A., Posey, D., Sullivan, J., Thurston, D., et al. (2008). *The College Curriculum in Higher Education.* Bethesda, MD: Academia Press.

Stovall, D. (2006). We can relate: Hip hop culture, critical pedagogy and the secondary classroom. *Urban Education, 41,* 585-602.

Stovall, D. (2008). Hip hop and social studies for critical analysis. In F. T. Roy (Ed.). *The Hip Hop Education Guidebook.* New York: Hip Hop Association.

Sullivan, R.E. (2003). Rap and race: It's got a nice beat, but what about the message? *Journal of Black Studies, 33,* 605-621).

Thompson, S., & Smith, D. (2005, Spring). Creating highly qualified teachers for urban schools. *The Professional Educator, 27*(1&2), 73-88.

U.S. Census Bureau (2008). Retrieved May 2, 2009 from http://www.census.gov.

Weiner, L. (2000, Fall). Research in the 90s: Implications for urban teacher preparation. *Review of Educational Research, 70*, 369-406.

Whisnant, E., Elliott, K., & Pynchon, S. (2005, July). A review of literature on beginning teacher induction. Center for Strengthening the Teaching Profession.

Wlodkowski, R.J. & Ginsberg, M.B. (1995). *Diversity and motivation.* San Francisco: Jossey-Bass.

Wolcott, H.F. (1994). *Transforming Qualitative Data.* Thousand Oaks, CA: Sage Publications.

Wong, H.K., & Wong, R.T. (2004) *The First Days of School.* Mountain View, CA: Harry K. Wong Publications.

Yates, L., Pelphrey, B.A., & Smith, P.A. (2008). An explanatory phenomenological study of African American male pre-service teachers at a historical black university in the mid-South. *National FORUM of Applied Education Research Journal, 21*(3). Retrieved July 21, 2008 from http://www.nationalforum.com/journals.

Thirst for knowledge the same way you thirst for air in your lungs, but until that point you are not ready. In order for these students to be free, they must thirst for knowledge like the last breath in their lungs. We have all of these books, all of these people from different parts of the world now. Knowledge is global. We learn from each other. Take advantage of the blessings we have in front of us.

David Banner
Speech at Claflin University
UNCF Empower Me Tour
October 2014

CAROL A. O'CONNOR, PHD

8 GOIN' WORLDWIDE

CAROL O'CONNOR IN ORGANIX: "GOIN' WORLDWIDE!"

Although hip-hop may most frequently be viewed as a dynamic entertainment platform, global hip-hop culture is a powerful force in education, and has emerged as distinct pedagogy. In the United States, more than 175 courses in hip-hop studies are offered at college and universities, and the use of this pedagogy in instruction at the K-12 level has been shown to produce greater student engagement and achievement.

The integration of music, lyrics, art, and dance into current educational practices in some other countries has been documented, but has only recently made inroads into Africa. This is especially interesting to note because although hip-hop first emerged in the Bronx, its roots undeniably trace themselves to the heart of Africa. Scholars have identified the source of hip-hop as the ancient tradition of what has become known as "freestylin'," which in the African context is spontaneous poetry set to a rhythmic pattern. The contemporary rhymes, beats and dance moves parallel those found in traditional cultures across the continent, but have taken on forms unique to each country.

To examine this phenomenon of a returning home, two countries are especially noteworthy; Ghana, on Africa's west coast, and Ethiopia on its east, offer glimpses into the evolution of this contemporary art form in two very different contexts. In Ghana, the term sankofa, refers to something of someone who has left, but then returns bringing something new.

Prior to the return of Ghanaian Reggie Rockstone to his homeland in the mid-1990s, Ghana had a flourishing genre of music called high life that was developed during the British colonial period. The hip-hop beats and rap style that Reggie brought from the US and England broadened the scope of Ghanaian music and the blend of these two forms became known as hip life music. Hip life artists such as Okyeame Kwame, who became known as the "rap docta" and others throughout the country gained fame with lyrics in local languages such twi, hausa, fanti and ga. Okyeame Kwame has retained his popularity for more than a decade.

During more recent years, a distinct hip hop style has gown, particularly in the capital city, Accra. Versatile artists like Kwaw Kese, Sarkodie, Tic Tac, C-Real, Grave Digga, and Scientific address social and personal issues, all set to deeply powerful beats. Although local languages are still used extensively in the music, English has become more widespread as these artists gain international attention. Samini, for example, who brands himself as the king of African dancehall, raps primarily in English, using his native ga for the hooks in songs such as "Where My Baby Dey." During more recent years, a distinct hip hop style has gown, particularly in the capital city, Accra. Versatile artists like Kwaw Kese, Sarkodie, Tic Tac, C-Real, Grave Digga, and Scientific address social and personal issues, all set to deeply powerful beats. Although local languages are still used extensively in the music, English has become more widespread as these artists gain international attention. Samini, for example, who brands himself as the king of African dancehall, raps primarily in English, using his native ga for the hooks in songs such as "Where My Baby Dey."

Some these artists have collaborated with artists in other countries. Kwaw Kese and Cape Coast artist Ambassadar, for example, have each recorded tracks with Mississippi rap artists P-Boy Stone and Stunna Mane. Kwaw also has a track called "War" with Wyclef Jean. "Telling Our Own Stories" international hip hop education conferences in Cape Coast, Accra and Mississippi – presented byRhyme-N-Reason Foundation – have showcased the talents of many of these artists in the context of scholarly presentations, workshops, and interactions with students and other artists.

On the other side of the African continent, Ethiopia presents a different picture altogether. Never colonized during its history, Ethiopia has remained more resistant to outside influences, although television, movies, music and other media have contributed to the formation of young people's identity and worldview. The best known rap artist in the country is Teddy Yo, who during a recent four-month performance gig in Dubai, collaborated on three tracks with Arab rap artist Wolfy tha Beast. Teddy brought the southern Ethiopian beats to these tracks which infused them with an identifiable form of solidity and vigor. Other Ethiopian hip-hop artists include the Gamo Boys, whose work reflects their southern roots, and Jungle Crew.

In the southern Ethiopian city of Hawassa, hip-hop culture is growing as like-minded educators, students and professional artists work together to apply the positive aspects of hip-hop culture to literacy projects. To date, a 20-page "Telling Our Own Stories" booklet of students' writing and art has been published; a presentation on hip-hop pedagogy was given at a national Ministry of Education in Addis; a visiting American professor educated faculty and students on the roots and relevance of hip-hop; an Ethiopian university lecturer has turned his attention to the impact of hip hop on the country's economic growth; Behulum Mengistu, Ethiopia's only graffiti artist, had his first exhibition using both English and Amharic writing styles; and Teddy Yo performed with young rappers at a concert to raise money for books and computers for an underserved local elementary school attended by some of the young performers.

Since the formal education systems in all countries seem resistant to change, these activities have been activated in the community and have begun to permeate into the regular curriculum. Leaderships skills are being fostered in the youth so that they can take full ownership of these projects, and use hip-hop culture to improve the lives of all.

Carol A. O'Connor, PhD
World Hip Hop Market
June 12, 2012

Don't worry about being a star, worry about doing good work, and all that will come to you.

Ice Cube

ABOUT THE AUTHOR

Carol O'Connor is the president of the Rhyme-N-Reason
Foundation, a non-profit organization that assists talented youth
from Jackson, Mississippi, to Cape Coast, Ghana, focusing on
education via hip-hop. Ms. O'Connor has spent most of her life in
education, teaching both high school and college level English
courses. Her PhD work at the Jackson State University focused on
hip-hop and education. She holds a B.A. in Philosophy from
University of California, Santa Barbara, and a M. Ed from the
University of Guam. She has lived all around the United States and
abroad in Ghana, Ethiopia, Dubai.

CAROL A. O'CONNOR, PHD

ABOUT THE EDITOR

Author, educator and publisher SaFiya D. Hoskins, PhD (Dr. Sa) is the owner of Ubiquitous Press with a catalogue as varied as children's books, academic research, poetry and non-fiction. She is the co-author of *Growth and Development for the Millennial Generation* with Wallace 'Gator' Bradley and Dr. Cornel West, an autobiographical treatise on race, religion and politics in Chicago. In addition to the nine books Dr. Sa has authored or edited, she has written over 60 articles for Harvard University's African American National Biography (Oxford University Press). Her research, *Faculty Perceptions of Racial Climate at HBCUs*, has been presented at international academic conferences. Dr. Sa has taught courses at several colleges and universities including Media Influence on American Culture; Mass Communications; Teamwork, Collaboration and Conflict Resolution. She was host of the talk radio show, *Beauty, Brains and the Bottom Line with Dr. Sa* on Radio One in Washington, DC and has worked with Def Jam Recordings, Inc.; BET; MHCDO, a nonprofit organization and in communications on Capitol Hill for Illinois Congressman Bobby Rush. She has appeared in two televisions commercials and on the Discovery Channel Network as Chef Emeril Lagasse's guest on Emeril Green. She earned a BA in Journalism/ Public Relations and an MA in Communication & Culture/ Organizational Communication both from Howard University. She also has a doctorate in Urban Higher Education/ Educational Leadership from Jackson State University. Dr. Sa resides in Washington, DC where she enjoys reading, jogging and studying law.

We hope you enjoyed this **UBIQUITOUS PRESS** publication.
If you would like to receive additional information, please contact:

UbiquitousPress@gmail.com

www.ubiquitouspressllc.com

Also on **UBIQUITOUS PRESS**:

<u>Nonfiction</u>

Murder to Excellence: Growth & Development for
the Millennial Generation
The Autobiography of Wallace 'Gator' Bradley

Murder to Excellence: Growth & Development for
the Millennial Generation
The Autobiography of Wallace 'Gator' Bradley
Study Guide

Invasion of Privacy: Hacking the Celebrity Code

White Faculty at HBCUs:
Perceptions of Racial Climate

Altruism at HBCUs

<u>Fiction</u>

The Adventures of Bouki and Rabby: Cottage in the Clouds

Binky: The Cutest Kitten Ever

Racing Thoughts

Made in the USA
Las Vegas, NV
23 January 2021